VISUAL C++® 6

FOR

DUMMIES®

Quick Reference

by Charles Wright

IDG Books Worldwide, Inc.
An International Data Group Company

Foster City, CA ✦ Chicago, IL ✦ Indianapolis, IN ✦ New York, NY

Visual C++® 6 For Dummies® Quick Reference

Published by
IDG Books Worldwide, Inc.
An International Data Group Company
919 E. Hillsdale Blvd.
Suite 400
Foster City, CA 94404
www.idgbooks.com (IDG Books Worldwide Web site)
www.dummies.com (Dummies Press Web site)

Library of Congress Catalog Card No.: 98-87103

ISBN: 0-7645-0373-1

Printed in the United States of America

10 9 8 7 6 5 4 3 2 1

1P/SX/QY/ZY/IN

Distributed in the United States by IDG Books Worldwide, Inc.

Distributed by Macmillan Canada for Canada; by Transworld Publishers Limited in the United Kingdom; by IDG Norge Books for Norway; by IDG Sweden Books for Sweden; by Woodslane Pty. Ltd. for Australia; by Woodslane (NZ) Ltd. for New Zealand; by Addison Wesley Longman Singapore Pte Ltd. for Singapore, Malaysia, Thailand, Indonesia and Korea; by Norma Comunicaciones S.A. for Colombia; by Intersoft for South Africa; by International Thomson Publishing for Germany, Austria and Switzerland; by Toppan Company Ltd. for Japan; by Distribuidora Cuspide for Argentina; by Livraria Cultura for Brazil; by Ediciencia S.A. for Ecuador; by Ediciones ZETA S.C.R. Ltda. for Peru; by WS Computer Publishing Corporation, Inc., for the Philippines; by Unalis Corporation for Taiwan; by Contemporanea de Ediciones for Venezuela; by Computer Book & Magazine Store for Puerto Rico; by Express Computer Distributors for the Caribbean and West Indies. Authorized Sales Agent: Anthony Rudkin Associates for the Middle East and North Africa.

For general information on IDG Books Worldwide's books in the U.S., please call our Consumer Customer Service department at 800-762-2974. For reseller information, including discounts and premium sales, please call our Reseller Customer Service department at 800-434-3422.

For information on where to purchase IDG Books Worldwide's books outside the U.S., please contact our International Sales department at 650-655-3200 or fax 650-655-3297.

For information on foreign language translations, please contact our Foreign & Subsidiary Rights department at 650-655-3021 or fax 650-655-3281.

For sales inquiries and special prices for bulk quantities, please contact our Sales department at 650-655-3200 or write to the address above.

For information on using IDG Books Worldwide's books in the classroom or for ordering examination copies, please contact our Educational Sales department at 800-434-2086 or fax 317-596-5499.

For press review copies, author interviews, or other publicity information, please contact our Public Relations department at 650-655-3000 or fax 650-655-3299.

For authorization to photocopy items for corporate, personal, or educational use, please contact Copyright Clearance Center, 222 Rosewood Drive, Danvers, MA 01923, or fax 978-750-4470.

is a trademark under exclusive license to IDG Books Worldwide, Inc., from International Data Group, Inc.

About the Author

Charles Wright is a 35-year veteran of the newspaper business, and has worked as a printer, reporter, editor, and columnist. He is currently the Systems Developer for the *Denver Post*. He has 20 years of experience as a C and C++ programmer on various platforms including UNIX, OS/2, Windows 95, and Windows NT.

Recently, Charles has developed a considerable body of unique code aimed at putting the contents of a newspaper on the World Wide Web.

ABOUT IDG BOOKS WORLDWIDE

Welcome to the world of IDG Books Worldwide.

IDG Books Worldwide, Inc., is a subsidiary of International Data Group, the world's largest publisher of computer-related information and the leading global provider of information services on information technology. IDG was founded more than 25 years ago and now employs more than 8,500 people worldwide. IDG publishes more than 275 computer publications in over 75 countries (see listing below). More than 90 million people read one or more IDG publications each month.

Launched in 1990, IDG Books Worldwide is today the #1 publisher of best-selling computer books in the United States. We are proud to have received eight awards from the Computer Press Association in recognition of editorial excellence and three from *Computer Currents'* First Annual Readers' Choice Awards. Our best-selling ...For Dummies® series has more than 50 million copies in print with translations in 38 languages. IDG Books Worldwide, through a joint venture with IDG's Hi-Tech Beijing, became the first U.S. publisher to publish a computer book in the People's Republic of China. In record time, IDG Books Worldwide has become the first choice for millions of readers around the world who want to learn how to better manage their businesses.

Our mission is simple: Every one of our books is designed to bring extra value and skill-building instructions to the reader. Our books are written by experts who understand and care about our readers. The knowledge base of our editorial staff comes from years of experience in publishing, education, and journalism — experience we use to produce books for the '90s. In short, we care about books, so we attract the best people. We devote special attention to details such as audience, interior design, use of icons, and illustrations. And because we use an efficient process of authoring, editing, and desktop publishing our books electronically, we can spend more time ensuring superior content and spend less time on the technicalities of making books.

You can count on our commitment to deliver high-quality books at competitive prices on topics you want to read about. At IDG Books Worldwide, we continue in the IDG tradition of delivering quality for more than 25 years. You'll find no better book on a subject than one from IDG Books Worldwide.

IDG
BOOKS
WORLDWIDE

John Kilcullen
CEO
IDG Books Worldwide, Inc.

Steven Berkowitz
President and Publisher
IDG Books Worldwide, Inc.

VIII
WINNER

Eighth Annual
Computer Press
Awards ≥1992

IX
WINNER

Ninth Annual
Computer Press
Awards ≥1993

X
WINNER

Tenth Annual
Computer Press
Awards ≥1994

XI
WINNER

Eleventh Annual
Computer Press
Awards ≥1995

Dedication

To my wife, Tammy, who has put up with my long work hours and kept me encouraged, and to The Bear, my Pomeranian pup, who keeps me entertained by playing with my computers as much as I do.

Acknowledgments

Thanks to the people at IDG Books, especially to Kyle Looper, who forced me to learn the discipline to write this book, to Patricia Pan, who kept my grammar from wandering too far, and to Maria Canton and Julio Sanchez, the technical editors who kept me from making some big mistakes.

Publisher's Acknowledgments

We're proud of this book; please register your comments through our IDG Books Worldwide Online Registration Form located at: http://my2cents.dummies.com.

Some of the people who helped bring this book to market include the following:

Acquisitions, Editorial, and Media Development

Project Editor: Kyle Looper

Senior Acquisitions Editor: Jill Pisoni

Copy Editor: Patricia Yuu Pan

Editorial Manager: Leah P. Cameron

Media Development Manager: Heather Heath Dismore

Editorial Assistant: Donna Love

Production

Project Coordinator: E. Shawn Aylsworth

Layout and Graphics: Lou Boudreau, Angela F. Hunckler, Drew R. Moore, Brent Savage, Kate Snell

Proofreaders: Kelli Botta, Nancy Price, Sandra Profant, Rebecca Senninger, Janet M. Withers

Indexer: Sharon Hilgenberg

General and Administrative

IDG Books Worldwide, Inc.: John Kilcullen, CEO; Steven Berkowitz, President and Publisher

IDG Books Technology Publishing: Brenda McLaughlin, Senior Vice President and Group Publisher

Dummies Technology Press and Dummies Editorial: Diane Graves Steele, Vice President and Associate Publisher; Mary Bednarek, Director of Acquisitions and Product Development; Kristin A. Cocks, Editorial Director

Dummies Trade Press: Kathleen A. Welton, Vice President and Publisher; Kevin Thornton, Acquisitions Manager

IDG Books Production for Dummies Press: Michael R. Britton, Vice President of Production and Creative Services; Beth Jenkins Roberts, Production Director; Cindy L. Phipps, Manager of Project Coordination, Production Proofreading, and Indexing; Kathie S. Schutte, Supervisor of Page Layout; Shelley Lea, Supervisor of Graphics and Design; Debbie J. Gates, Production Systems Specialist; Robert Springer, Supervisor of Proofreading; Debbie Stailey, Special Projects Coordinator; Tony Augsburger, Supervisor of Reprints and Bluelines

Dummies Packaging and Book Design: Robin Seaman, Creative Director; Jocelyn Kelaita, Product Packaging Coordinator; Kavish + Kavish, Cover Design

♦

The publisher would like to give special thanks to Patrick J. McGovern, without whom this book would not have been possible.

♦

Table of Contents

Part IV: The Resource Workshop 61

Part V: The Help Workshop 93

Part VI: Constants, Arrays, and Variables... 113

Part VII: Decision-Making Statements 129

How to Use This Book

You're a busy person — much too busy to spend your precious time reading a long treatise on Visual C++. You already know something about programming, and you don't need me to tell you how to use loops and conditional statements in your code. What you *do* need to know is how Visual C++ can help you with Windows programming and maybe a reminder now and then of how the syntax of various C++ statements work and what those statements accomplish. And you want to get that information *fast*.

Well, you've come to the right place. *Visual C++ For Dummies Quick Reference* is specifically designed to give you the information you need as quickly as possible so that you can get back to creating cool Windows applications with Visual C++. Keep this handy little reference right by your computer for those times during marathon coding sessions when you wonder what a particular menu item means or for when you need a quick fix on a bit of C++ syntax.

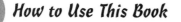

How This Book Is Organized

This book is composed of 11 parts, each of which covers a specific area of the Visual C++ program or Visual C++ programming. To find particular information on a Visual C++ subject, first figure out what classification it falls under, and then look at the alphabetical listings in that part. For example, if you want to find out how to declare a pointer in Visual C++, go to the part on Constants, Arrays, and Variables, look alphabetically until you get to pointers, and there it is!

The parts of this book are organized by subject matter, as follows:

Part I: Getting to Know Visual C++: In this part you can get your feet wet with the Visual C++ Integrated Development Environment, including customizing the environment, using and customizing toolbars, and starting Visual C++.

Part II: Creating a New Application: This part tells you how Visual C++ makes it easy to create Windows applications. In fact, you can create a working Windows application in minutes using the steps detailed in this part.

Part III: Building and Debugging a Project: This part provides you with what you need to know to add code to your application and debug that code.

Part IV: The Resource Workshop: The resource workshop is the part of Visual C++ where you add ways for the user to interact with your program (buttons, dialog boxes, and so on) and where you tell your program how to handle the messages created by all those user clicks and keystrokes.

Part V: The Help Workshop: Because the job's not over 'til the paperwork's done, you can find help for creating help files in this chapter. The work you do in creating a help file can really pay off in terms of the time you don't lose answering users' questions later.

Part VI: Constants, Arrays, and Variables: This part helps you out with the syntax for declaring constants, arrays, and various variables in Visual C++.

Part VII: Decision-Making Statements: This part tells you about the use and syntax of the four decision-making statements in Visual C++: `if`, `for`, `while`, and `switch`.

Part VIII: Classes: Classes allow you to write reusable object-oriented code. This part tells you the syntax for working with classes.

Part IX: Operators: This part can refresh your memory about how operators work in C++.

Part X: Taking Advantage of Windows: From splash screens to Registry entries, this part tells you about using features of Windows in your programs.

Part XI: The Microsoft Foundation Class: This part gives points out some aspects of the Microsoft Foundation Class — reusable code that comes with Visual C++.

Glossary: Techie Talk: Look up unfamiliar words in this part.

Conventions Used in This Book

I show code elements, such as variable names, commands, collections, controls, methods, variables, and so on, in this way: myCode. If the code extends beyond one line, you'll see something like the following code fragment:

```
for (i = 1; i < 5; i++)
    {//do something
    ...
    };
```

For placeholder code that you need to change, I use italics. For example:

```
class classname
```

In this case, you would put the name of the class you are declaring in place of the text classname.

The Icon Crew

Look for the following icons in the margins of the parts that follow to call special attention to the text it accompanies. The meanings of these icons are as follows:

This icon points out a particular hoop that you can make Visual C++ jump through and save yourself some programming hassle.

This icon points out the quickest way to get something done in Visual C++.

Ignore text marked with this little bomb at your own peril!

This icon points out something that will have you scratching your head and chuckling.

This icon provides a sample that illustrates the use of a particular element.

This icon points you toward another book for a more detailed explanation than I give you here.

This icon tells you where to go to get the syntax for a particular bit of code.

Part 1

Getting to Know Visual C++

Suppose you were given the chance to build the C++ development environment you wanted. What would you put in it? Perhaps a way to build starter program files for even the most complex projects without having to gather skeleton program files and recode them. Or maybe a panel that shows all the files, classes, variables, and resource objects in your program at a glance. Or perhaps you'd consider including a method to add new classes to your program, automatically create the header file definitions, and build basic source code files with constructors and destructors.

Well, you can go on dreaming, but if you haven't guessed yet, that wish list and more describes Microsoft's Visual C++ Version 6.0 Integrated Development Environment (IDE).

In this part . . .

✔ **Customizing the Developer's workshop**

✔ **Customizing toolbars**

✔ **Modifying the Tools menu**

✔ **Meeting the wizards**

✔ **Starting Visual C++**

✔ **Watching the workshop windows**

✔ **Reading the workshop menus**

Customizing the Developer's Workshop

Visual C++ is part of the Microsoft Developer's Workshop. As busy as the workshop frame seems when you first start it up, it contains only a portion of the toolbars, menus, and windows that are available to you while developing a program.

The workshop isn't a static place. The screen changes according to what you're doing — whether editing a program file, debugging code, or building resources. On top of that, you can move toolbars and windows, placing them where they are most effective for you. You can even customize some of the individual windows and build your own toolbars. Microsoft truly designed this to be a *developer's workshop*.

You may want to start out using the workshop as it first appears. As you gain more experience, you discover the most useful toolbars and the handiest places on the screen to have them. Take the default configuration, for example: The build and debug toolbars are on opposite sides of the screen, so you need to slide the mouse a long way to start a debug session and to pause it. A more convenient approach is to move the toolbars next to each other or even to build your own toolbar containing these two buttons.

Before you begin customizing, however, a word of caution is in order. Not everything is as simple as it looks, but that's what makes the workshop so flexible. Options, for example, is a single word on a menu, yet it conjures up a 10-tab dialog box that, in other circumstances, could be considered an application in itself.

The Tools and Menu dialog boxes enable you to customize the tools and menus of the workshop. You can add or delete menus and menu items, modify existing toolbars or create new ones, or add your custom tools to the Tools menu.

You access the Tools and Menu dialog boxes by choosing either Tools⇨Customize or Tools⇨Options. If you need immediate help, click the ? button and then a button, option, or check box. The following minitable shows the tasks you can do with these tools:

Dialog Box	Tab	What You Can Do
Customize	Commands	Add commands, including toolbar commands, to menus and toolbars
Customize	Toolbars	Set which toolbars are visible, enable tool tips and shortcut keys, enable large icons on toolbars
Customize	Tools	Add commands to or delete commands from the Tools menu

Dialog Box	*Tab*	*What You Can Do*
Customize	Keyboard	Modify keyboard shortcut keys to a command or assign shortcut keys to commands that don't have shortcuts
Customize	Add-Ins and Macro Files	Enable and disable add-ins and macro files
Options	Editor	Set editor and file save options
Options	Tabs	Set the tab stops and options for the various file types used in the IDE (the smart indent options are available only for C/C++ files and only if you select the Smart option under Auto Indent)
Options	Debug	Set the display and behavior options for the debugging process (Of interest here is the Just-in-Time Debugging option. Selecting this box inserts information for Windows to start up the IDE and begin debugging the program when it encounters an error.)
Options	Compatibility	Set the text editor to emulate the Brief editor, EPSILON editor, or the old Visual C++ 2.0 editor (if you're new to programming, stick with the default Developer Studio editor)
Options	Build	Specify settings for makefiles, which are used when building a program from the command line (As long as you won't stay within the IDE, you won't need to worry about makefiles. You can select the Write Build Log option to cause Visual C++ to create a log that shows the options and build sequence used to put together your programs.)
Options	Directories	Specify where the IDE looks for various types of files during the project editing/build sequence
Options	Workspace	Set the default behavior of the IDE on startup (the Docking Views window lets you determine whether certain window frame elements are to be docked or not)
Options	Macro	Select how the Developer Studio handles macro files that you have changed since they last ran
Options	Format	Customize the appearance of the various windows in the IDE
Options	InfoViewer	Sets display options for the InfoViewer window (the font size setting is useful, especially after a bleary-eyed night of debugging)

Customizing Toolbars

You can create, edit, or delete toolbars from the Visual C++ IDE to make the workshop reflect the way you work.

Toolbars you create are custom toolbars. Any changes you make to a custom toolbar are permanent.

Adding tools to a toolbar

You can add tools to any toolbar, including the standard toolbars. If you want to add a tool to a toolbar, follow these steps:

1. Choose Tools⇨Customize. Click the Toolbars tab.

2. Make sure the toolbar is visible by putting a check mark in the box next to it.

3. Click the Commands tab.

4. Select the category that contains the toolbar items you want to add.

5. Click the appropriate button and drag it to the toolbar. Release the mouse button to drop the tool onto the bar.

Creating a toolbar

Follow these steps to create a custom toolbar:

1. Choose Tools⇨Customize. The dialog box that appears contains a check box for Large buttons. This option applies to all the buttons on the frame.

2. Choose the Toolbars tab. The toolbars with a check mark next to them are already visible on the screen.

3. Click New and give your toolbar a name.

4. Click OK. An empty toolbar appears in the upper-left corner of the Workshop. You may have to move the Customize dialog box out of the way to see it.

5. Click the Commands tab.

6. From the category list, select the tool you want with the mouse and drag it to where you want it to appear on your new toolbar. Release the mouse.

 • To reposition a tool, click the button and drag it to the new position. Release the mouse.

 • To remove a tool from the toolbar, click the button, drag it to an open area off the toolbar, and release the mouse. You can't undo a removal; to put a tool back on the toolbar, repeat the above step.

7. Click Close. The toolbar is left floating. To dock it, drag the toolbar and drop it on the frame.

Deleting a toolbar

You can delete any custom toolbar. Although you may modify the standard toolbars, you may not delete them.

To delete a toolbar, follow these steps:

1. Choose Tools⇨Customize.

2. Click the Toolbars tab.

3. Select the toolbar you want to delete, and click Delete. You can't undo a toolbar delete, so make sure you don't need it anymore.

Remember: The Delete button is disabled for standard toolbars.

Displaying or hiding a toolbar

Right-click on any toolbar to show the toolbar menu where you can show or hide any of the toolbars by selecting or deselecting the toolbar.

Removing tools from a toolbar

To remove a tool from any toolbar, follow these steps:

1. Hold down the Alt key and click on the tool you want to remove. You don't have to open the Customize dialog box to do this.

2. Drag the tool over an open area of the edit window and release the mouse. Dropping the tool over another toolbar adds it to that toolbar.

Renaming a toolbar

The toolbar name is visible only when the toolbar is undocked. You can rename toolbars by doing the following:

1. Choose Tools⇨Customize and click the Toolbars tab.

2. Select the toolbar you want to rename and type its new name in the edit box below the list.

Resetting a toolbar

You can reset a standard toolbar to its original state when you no longer need the changes. Just follow these steps:

1. Choose Tools⇨Customize from the menu, and then open the Toolbars property page.

2. Select the toolbar you want to restore.

3. Click Reset. The toolbar restores to its default state. To reset all the toolbars, click the Reset All button.

Menus

You find only one menu bar on the Workshop frame, and you can't hide it — unless you're editing a file in full-screen mode. By default, it appears at the top of the workshop frame. Many menus remain hidden until you need them. If I covered all of these menus and their multitude of variations, this book wouldn't be a quick reference anymore. I address the main menu in the following table and try to give an overview of the most useful hidden menus. I cover many other menus in other sections. For example, The Resource Workshop details the pop-ups on the Resource.

Menu	*Submenu Options*
File	Gives access to the New property sheet; open, save, and close files and workspaces; printer functions and Workshop exit
Edit	Cut, copy, paste, and undo functions; find and replace; bookmarks; access to breakpoints. The Advanced submenu offers selections for formatting, incremental searches, and changing the case of selected text. Microsoft has had entabbing and untabbing functions in IDEs for as long as I can remember; you find them here.
View	Access to Script and Class wizards; resource symbols and include files; full-screen edit mode; show workspace, InfoView, output, and debug windows; file properties
Insert	Insert various objects such as classes, resource objects, files, ATL objects
Project	Project functions; set dependencies; access to Setup dialog box
Build	Compiler and debugger functions; access to configurations and profile dialog boxes
Tools	Browser functions; run external programs used as tools; access to Customize and Options dialog boxes
Window	Window functions and list
Help	InfoViewer access; tips; technical help

You can access some useful context menus by right-clicking the mouse at certain locations:

✦ Right-click on a blank area of a source or header file to access the cut, copy, and paste functions; the ClassWizard; and the Properties dialog box for the file.

✦ Right-click on a word to go to the definition or reference for the word. If the word is a function name, you may jump to the definition or declaration — assuming you have browsing enabled. If browsing isn't enabled, you get a chance to enable it from this menu.

✦ Right-click on resource objects to get access to functions that depend upon the object.

Customizing the Tools menu

You can add or delete programs to and from the Tools menu.

To add a program to the Tools menu:

1. Choose Tools⇨Customize. Click the Tools tab.

2. Double-click the open rectangle at the bottom of the tool list.

3. Type the tool name. Inserting an ampersand (&) before a letter makes it the accelerator key.

4. Press the tab key to activate the edit boxes below the list.

5. In the Command box, type the program name. Click the button to the right (labeled "...") to open a file search.

6. In the Arguments box, type in any parameters the tool needs. Press the arrow to the right to get a list of Developer Studio variables. If the arguments vary with each run, check the Prompt for Arguments box at the bottom of the dialog.

7. In the Initial Directory box, type the working directory of the tool. Press the button to the right to get a list of directories used in the current project.

8. Select the Use Output Window check box at the bottom and you then see a tab appear in the output window. Selecting this check box allows you to see the program's output in a window.

9. Close the dialog box and test the tool.

To delete a program from the tools menu, follow these steps:

1. Choose Tools⇨Customize⇨Tools tab.

2. Select the tool you want to remove from the menu.

3. Click the Delete tool (the red X just above the tool list). The tool is removed. If the tool was writing to the output window, the tab on the output window is removed as well.

The wizard bar action menu

The wizard bar action menu is part of a warp-drive control system that lets you zip around your application and perform super-programmer feats.

See also "The Wizard Bar" in Part II.

Project Wizards

The application wizards of Visual C++ help you to create many types of applications, as shown in the following table. Create an application by following these steps:

1. Choose File⇨New, or press Ctrl+N, to summon the dialog box. This dialog box has tabs for creating files, projects, workspaces, and ActiveX documents.

2. If you don't have a project open in the workspace, the dialog box opens on the Projects tab; otherwise, it opens on the Files tab. In the latter case, click the Projects tab. You can see a list of wizards and the types of applications you can create as shown in the figure below.

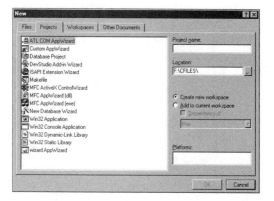

In addition to the wizards, the Projects tab also has options to set up standard Windows applications and libraries. Unlike the MFC wizards, these options don't generate any program code. They build only the workspace files.

Wizard Name	Purpose
MFC ActiveX ControlWizard	Guides you through the steps of setting up an ActiveX control, and then creates the files you need — object description language (.ODL) and source, header, and resource files.
MFC AppWizard	Helps you through the steps of creating a new application. This is your main wizard for most applications.
ATL-COM AppWizard	The Active Template Library is a set of template-based classes that permit you to create small but efficient Component Object Model objects, the basis of ActiveX. This wizard takes you through the process of creating an ATL application.

Wizard Name	Purpose
Custom AppWizard	Walks you through the steps of creating your own wizard. You can create your own custom wizard from scratch, make an existing project into a wizard, or opt to add your own steps to the AppWizards.
ISAPI Extension Wizard	This guy takes you through the steps of creating an Internet Server Application Programming Interface (ISAPI) extension or filter. ISAPI is an alternative to the Common Gateway Interface (CGI) programs.

Many of these wizards are beyond the scope of this book, but Visual C++ was written for programmers of all levels, and you may eventually find a need for them. For this book, however, you'll concentrate on the MFC wizards for creating applications and libraries.

Starting Visual C++

Visual C++ is part of the Developer Studio, which you can access from the Start Menu. Even if you have no other Developer Studio products installed, the menu shows a number of tools depending upon the options you selected at installation time.

Creating a desktop icon

If you use Visual C++ often, you may want to create a desktop icon for it. This saves you the time of stepping through the Start menu.

Follow these steps to create a desktop icon:

1. Double-click the My Computer icon on the desktop, and then double-click the drive on which you've installed Visual C++.

2. Navigate through the folders until you reach the program file folder.

If you used the default folder during the installation, the sequence is DevStudio⇨SharedIDE⇨bin. Find the icon for MSDEV.EXE in this folder.

3. *Right-click* on this icon, and hold the mouse button down. Drag the icon out of the folder to someplace on your desktop.

4. Release the right mouse button. From the menu that pops up, select the menu option Create Shortcut(s) Here.

Anytime you want to run Visual C++, just double-click on the desktop icon.

Running Visual C++ from the Start menu

To start Visual C++ from the Start menu, choose Start⇨Programs⇨
Microsoft Visual C++ 6.0⇨Microsoft Visual C++ 6.0.

Window Watching

Technically, every object in the IDE is a window — the title bar,
individual toolbar buttons, the Workspace, and so on — with a
particular control applied to it. Practically, however, you refer to a
window as an object that displays information that can vary
according to what you do with the data.

Using that definition, three windows appear in the IDE when you
first start it up, as shown in the following figure.

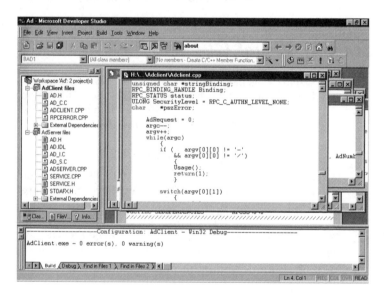

✦ **The Editing window.** This is the MDI (multiple document
interface) client area and is the largest area in the middle of
the IDE. When you open a source file or InfoViewer topic, a
child window containing data for that object appears in this
area. Notice that a child window gets clipped when a portion
of the window moves outside the client area. Dialog boxes
may appear in this area, but they aren't MDI child windows
and aren't clipped by moving them out of the Editing window.

+ **The Workspace window.** Each of the four panels is a separate window containing tree views of the program elements on the tab label. This window normally appears on the left side of the frame below the menus and toolbars. Click the tabs at the bottom to select a view.

+ **The Output window.** This window, normally at the very bottom of the frame, contains a tab control to choose Find in Files, build, and debug windows. If you've added a tool and specified that it should write to the Output window, a tab for the tool appears.

Remember: In addition, the IDE contains several other windows that are invisible until you start debugging a program. See Part III for more on building and debugging a project.

The Editing window

The large area in the middle of the workshop is where you can edit your source files. If you consider the workshop itself an application (after all, it was created with earlier versions of the workshop), this area technically is the MDI client window. Experiment with moving and resizing windows using the minimize and maximize tools. If you create an MDI application, your data windows behave in the same way.

Exploring the Workspace window

The Developers Studio organizes the elements of your program and displays them in the Workspace window. The actual panels that you see depend on the type of project you have open. You select a panel by clicking on its tab at the bottom of the window.

If the Workspace isn't already visible, open it by clicking the Workspace button on the toolbar. You also can open the workspace by choosing <u>V</u>iew⇨Workspace or by pressing Alt+0.

For a C++ project, at least four panels are available to you:

✦ **Class View.** Lists the classes in your project and their member functions and variables. Double-click on a class name to open the file that contains the class definition. Double-click on a member function to open the file containing the function, and position the cursor at its definition.

✦ **File View.** Lists the files you included in your project by category (source, header, resource, and so on). Expanding a category reveals a list of files, and you may go directly to that file by double-clicking it. You can also invoke the Project Setting dialog box by right-clicking any item and selecting Settings from the popup menu. You can invoke resource tools by double-clicking a resource file.

✦ **Info View.** This panel is an information storehouse and is a good starting place for help. Info View contains information on Microsoft products, the developers network, and programming tools. Here you find listings for tools, a Visual C++ reference, software development kit documentation, and access to the developer network.

✦ **Resource View.** Resources are listed by object type. Expanding a type reveals the objects in your program. You can invoke the Resource Workshop from this panel or any of the resource tools. Double-clicking an object opens the object in a resource editor. Right-clicking opens a menu that lets you insert new objects.

Remember: If you don't have a workspace open, only the Info View panel is visible.

The Workspace window is a dockable object. Normally, the Workspace window is on the left side of the screen, but you can move it to any location you want or even leave it unattached. Grab the double line at the top with the left mouse button, and drag the window to any place on the frame. Release the mouse button, and the window docks.

You can hide any of the four panels by right-clicking on a tab and selecting from the pop-up menu. You can hide any three of the four panels. To restore a panel, right-click on a tab, and then select the panel you want to show.

Undocking the Workspace Window makes it appear as another child window in the editing window. This method is a convenient way to quickly expand the editing area and still have the workspace panels available. To undock the Workspace Window, right-click on any area in the window (including on a tab) and select Docking View.

The Output window

The Output window is a tab control window where the workshop writes messages to you and displays the result of Find In Files searches. You can add tabs to the Output window by adding your own tools to the Tools menu and specifying that the output should go to the Output window. Normally, however, the window contains four tabs:

+ **Build.** This window shows the results of compiling and linking your program. Watch this window for any errors in the compile. Double-clicking on an error message opens the source window and places the cursor on the line containing the error.

+ **Debug.** Watch this window after a debugging session for any messages from the debugger. Problems that don't necessarily stop the program are noted in this window. In Part III, which covers building and debugging a project, you discover how to write your own debug messages to this window.

+ **Find In Files 1 and Find In Files 2.** These panels display the results of running the Find In Files command. Normally, the command writes the results to Find In Files 1, but you may use the second panel by checkmarking the Output to Pane 2 box in the Find In Files dialog box.

Workspace pop-ups

What happens in Workspace pop-ups depends on which panel you have open and what is under the mouse cursor.

1. Right-click on the top-level line (the classes) on the ClassView panel. You get a menu to set the selected project as the active project, add a new class (*not* the ClassWizard), create a new ATL object, and create a folder.

2. Right-click on the same line on the ResourceView panel for access to the Resource Includes dialog box and a window to edit resource symbols. You also have options to save the resource file and add or import resource objects.

3. On the files page, the topmost item is the workspace itself; options here are to add a project to the workspace or to insert a project into the workspace. Click on a project name to get a project menu.

Creating a New Application

When you have a good idea for a program, you want to get right into writing it. But creating a Windows application can be a tedious process. Before you get into making your program perform, a lot of code is necessary just to create a window, set up menus, and do other chores to placate the operating system. Many programmers have learned to keep a skeleton (program, that is) or two in the closet and drag them out for just this purpose. The good news is that Windows libraries such as the Microsoft Foundation Class (MFC) put most of that startup code into library form, and the IDE goes a step farther: Wizards in the IDE generate most of the remaining startup code for you, which means you can create a working application in minutes. You can get right into creating the program you want.

In this part . . .

- ✔ **Adding files to a project**
- ✔ **Applications**
- ✔ **Changing project settings**
- ✔ **Compiling and running a program**
- ✔ **Creating new applications**
- ✔ **Saving your work**

Adding Files to a Project

The wizards of Visual C++ create most of the files your project needs. The MFC AppWizard creates the startup files, and as you add classes to your project, the ClassWizard creates the header and source files for the classes.

From time to time, however, you may need to add new or existing files to your project that the wizards can't handle.

Creating and adding new files

Not all files can be handled by the wizards. You may want to create a program file to hold utility routines that are not a member of any class. For example, the callback routines for list controls are better handled outside a class, and you may want to place these in a separate program file and include a header file to declare the functions.

To create a new file and add it to your project:

1. Select File➪New, and then click the Files tab.

2. Select the type of file you want to create.

3. Select the Add to Project check box at the upper right of the dialog box, and give your file a name in the Project Name edit box.

4. Click OK. Visual C++ creates the file and adds it to your project.

Adding existing files

You can add files from any drive or directory to your project. This is particularly handy as you develop utility routines to handle various functions; you don't have to copy them into your project directory to include them in your program.

To add an existing file to your project:

1. Choose Project➪Add to Project ➪Files.

2. Navigate through the file dialog to find the file you want to add.

Files need not be in the project directory, nor even on the same drive.

Applications

An application is the result of your programming efforts. The application isn't necessarily limited to the program itself, but it can include help files, any support libraries you've developed to support the main program, or any other elements needed by the main program. Applications generally are dialog- or document-based, but you can mix the types.

Dialog-based applications

If you don't want your Windows application to create a main window, the AppWizard provides a simple way to launch a dialog box on startup. You need only select the Dialog Based option when you start the wizard.

See also "Creating Applications" in this part for more on how to use the AppWizard to create a dialog-based application.

Document applications

Most Windows applications involve opening a main window in which you create one or more child windows to display data, whether text or a database record in a form. These applications are considered *document based*.

Options for document-based applications include

✦ **Single Document Interface (SDI).** Only one document may be open for editing or creating at a time.

✦ **Multiple Document Interface (MDI).** Originally specified by IBM, this interface involves creating a client class to manage the documents. MFC contains full support for MDI, and the MFC AppWizard handles the task of setting up the client and views.

See also "Creating Applications" in this part for steps to create an application using the MFC AppWizard.

Compiling and Running a Program

As your project develops, you want to compile and test it often. Compiling involves changing your source code into instructions the computer can understand. The Visual C++ compiler handles this task.

To compile your project, press the Build button on either the Build toolbar or Build Minibar toolbar or hit F7. The Build tab at the bottom of the display opens and shows you the progress of the compilation.

To compile a single program file, select it in the editor; then press the "Compile" button on the toolbar. You also may press Ctrl+F7 to compile a selected file.

To run your compiled program, press the Go button on the toolbar or press F5. If any files have been modified since the last compile, the IDE asks whether you want to rebuild the executable file. The program file loads into memory, and the IDE executes it.

See also "Building and Debugging a Project" in Part III.

Creating Applications

Visual C++ is an application-oriented development environment. You can create several types of programs by using the application wizards. You generally base applications on the Microsoft Foundation Class (MFC) and create them using the MFC AppWizard. For any type project, however, the beginning steps are the same.

To create a new Windows application in Visual C++ using the Application Wizards, perform the following steps:

1. Choose File⇨New, or type Ctrl+N. If you don't already have a workspace or project open, Visual C++ opens the Projects page by default.

2. Select the wizard for the application type you want to create. For most applications, you use the MFC AppWizard (.exe).

3. Type a project name. As you type a name, the wizard builds a default path in the Location box. You can change the location after you type the name of the project. If this is a new project and you haven't opened a workspace, the wizard selects the Create New Workspace radio button and disables the Add to Current Workspace radio button.

4. Select a platform for which the project will be built. For Windows 9x projects, select only Win32.

5. Click OK.

> *See also* "MFC AppWizard" in this part for the settings and information you need to give the MFC AppWizard.

> *See also* "Building and Debugging a Project" in Part III.

Dynamic Link Libraries

DLLs are ready-to-run libraries a program can summon at will. If you have code that more than one program uses, such as database access, you can build a DLL and load it at run time.

The wizard does not create source code files for dynamic link libraries that are not based on MFC: The wizard only creates the project files.

The wizard treats MFC-based libraries differently: The wizard does generate some base code, but it needs some information from you on what to include. To build an MFC DLL:

1. Select MFC AppWizard (.dll) from the Projects tab of the New dialog box.

2. Type a name for the project into the Project Name text box, and click OK.

3. Choose your options for DLL type from the following:

- **Regular DLL with MFC Statically Linked.** Links the MFC library to your code at build time. Your code is available to any Win32 or MFC application.

  Note: This option is available only in the Professional and Enterprise editions.

- **Regular DLL Using Shared MFC DLL.** The default. Your code uses the MFC DLL. This option reduces the size and memory requirements of your code. Your DLL must include a CWinApp function, but it doesn't handle messages.

- **MFC Extension DLL (using shared MFC DLL).** Only applications that use the MFC as a shared library can use calls in this type of DLL. You must provide a DllMain function but no CWinApp function.

4. Select the features you want in your library. Your options are

- **Automation.** Causes the wizard to create an ODL (object description language) file and to include OLE functions

- **Windows Sockets.** Allows you to write programs that operate over TCP/IP networks

5. Check whether you want the wizard to include comments in the source files. Select the Yes, Please radio button or the No, Thank You radio button.

MFC AppWizard

Document- and dialog-based MFC applications use the same wizard, the MFC AppWizard. The wizard for dialog-based MFC applications doesn't show a couple of screens that you get with the document-based MFC AppWizard and limits available features in Step 4.

Microsoft has put a lot of effort into this wizard, which can handle the bulk of Windows applications. The wizard needs a lot of information from you, but at the end it creates tons of code based on your responses.

The options offered by the wizard steps are particularly important in the development of your program, and you should spend some time understanding the wizard. Many project options can be changed later, but some of them are settled finally in these steps. For example, you can always add a rich edit control later, but it's more trouble than it's worth to switch from a single-document to a multidocument interface.

Step 1: Selecting an application type

On the first page, select the type of application you are preparing.

♦ **Single Document.** An application of this type allows a user to work on only one document at a time. To work on a second, the user has to close the first document.

♦ **Multiple Document.** A user can open several documents at a time — even of different types, depending upon the "views" you put in your project — without having to close others. When you select this option, the AppWizard generates a client class, and the document windows become child windows of the client.

♦ **Dialog Based.** This type of application doesn't include a main window or frame. If you choose this type, the wizard steps are not the same as those for a document-based application.

Select a language for your application on this page. If you look in the VC\MFC\Include subfolder where you installed Visual C++, you see a number of "l.xxx" folders. These contain basic resources in various languages that the wizard uses to prepare your application. If you select "French," the wizard draws from the "L.FRA" folder, and your resources get prepared in French. "File" on the menu becomes *Fichier,* and *New* under *Fichier* becomes *Nouveau.* As a *tuyauteux d'ordinateur* (computer hacker), you may want to try out different languages. You'll have to write other resources in the proper language; the IDE doesn't translate them.

Note: If this is a dialog-based application, the wizard skips Steps 2 and 3. Go on to Step 4.

Step 2: Adding database support

The second page contains options to include database support for your application. Check the radio button for the option you want.

+ **None.** The AppWizard does not include files for database support.

+ **Header Files Only.** This is the basic level of support. The wizard creates a header file (afxdb.h) and includes the link libraries in the compile, but it does not create any database classes.

+ **Database View Without File Support.** Select this option to ask the wizard to include header files, a record view, link libraries, and a recordset in the program it creates. Selecting this option enables the Source button beneath it, and you must specify the data source.

+ **Database View With File Support.** The same as the previous option except the wizard includes support for serialization. Database programs generally operate on records and do not require serialization. A key concept of serialization, however, is that an object includes procedures to read and write its own state, and it could be applied to database records.

If you select either of the last two options, you have to specify the data source, Open Database Connectivity (ODBC) or Data Access Objects (DAO). These topics are beyond the scope of this book, but a number of books about these topics are available.

Step 3: Using compound documents

The third page contains options for compound document support (a new way of saying OLE).

+ **None:** The wizard generates no compound document support. You may not use `CRichEditView` as the base view class.

+ **Container:** Allows you to include nontext files, such as .AVI, .WAV, or .BMP, in a document and to summon the proper application when they are opened from your program. This is the minimum support required for rich edit views.

+ **Mini-server:** Select this option if you want your application to only be able to create and manage compound document items. This type of application cannot run alone. A container-type program calls a miniserver application to handle files with a particular extension or characteristic.

+ **Full server:** You can use this type of program to perform tasks such as file editing, but a container-type application can also call this type of program to handle particular files.

✦ **Both container and server:** This type of application lets your application be both a server for other applications and a container to hold objects that other applications handle. With this type application you can, for example, create a text document that includes imbedded .AVI or .WAV files. Icons represent the objects in the document, and selecting one of the icons invokes the server for that object. You can use this option with the rich edit control.

If you plan to use one of the last three options, I strongly recommend additional reading on OLE and compound documents. Also, if you check the "ActiveX" document server, I recommend *ActiveX Controls Inside Out* by Adam Denning (Microsoft Press).

Remember: Microsoft is very serious about pushing OLE. If you are writing an application to market and you want the Windows 9*x* seal, you have to provide some level of *OLE* support. On the plus side, the wizard generates a lot of code to get you started.

Step 4: Adding features to your application

Select the features you want the wizard to add to your application. These include toolbars and the ability to print your documents. This is the most involved page and includes a two-page popup tab.

Note: If this is a dialog-based application, your only choices are an About Box, Context-Sensitive Help, and 3D Controls. (The wizard automatically creates an About box for document applications.)

✦ **Docking toolbar.** Adds a default toolbar to your application. The bar includes buttons for creating a new document; opening and saving files; using the cut, copy, and paste edit functions; displaying the About box; and entering Help mode. You also get a menu item to hide or display the toolbar.

✦ **Initial status bar.** Adds a status bar and message line to the bottom of the application window frame. The status bar contains indicators for the NUM LOCK, SCROLL LOCK, and CAPS LOCK keys. The status bar includes a message window for extended Help tips or any other message you want to write.

✦ **Print and print preview.** Causes the wizard to add code to handle print, print setup, and print preview commands. These items also are added to the menu. The wizard adds a Print button to the toolbar, but not a Print Preview button.

✦ **Context-sensitive help.** Creates a set of Help files for context-sensitive help. This option requires the Help compiler, which comes with Visual C++.

See also Part IV for more on help.

✦ **3D controls.** Gives a three-dimensional shading to the program's user interface.

This page also contains options for the Windows Open Services Architecture (WOSA). Your options are

✦ **MAPI.** The Messaging Applications Programming Interface is a set of functions that gives programs the ability to create, store, manipulate, and transfer messages, which may include entire files. MAPI support is added to the `CDocument` class.

✦ **Windows Sockets.** You need this when you write programs that communicate over a network. Windows sockets allow you to communicate over TCP/IP networks, such as the Internet.

Note: If this is a dialog-based application, your only choice is Windows Sockets.

Dialog-based application features end here. If you are creating a dialog-based application, use the Title edit box to give your dialog box a title and go to Step 5.

Step 4 has two other important items. The How Many Files Would You Like on Your Recent File List text box controls the size of the *Most Recently Used (MRU)* list. If you enter a value here, the wizard creates code to save the most recently opened files in the Windows Registry under the *HKEY_USERS* key. The use of the *HKEY_USERS* key permits different users of your application on the same computer to see their own MRUs, depending upon the user name they typed when starting Windows. If you don't want an MRU list, set this to 0.

More Step 4: Document template strings

The final item on Step 4 is the Advanced button, which summons the Advanced Options dialog. This dialog controls the labels and display in various elements of your application. The first page sets up the document template for your application.

You can create multiple templates in your code, but the wizard contains a dialog item for only the first one. The options for the template are

✦ **File extension.** The default extension for files created by the application. Entering an extension here allows Explorer to print your program's documents without launching your application when a user drags and drops a file of this type over a printer icon. When entering an extension, remember that Windows 9*x* is not limited to three characters.

✦ **File type ID.** The ID used to label your document type in the *HKEY_CLASSES_ROOT* key of the Windows Registry. It can't contain any spaces or punctuation marks other than a period. The Registry information contains items such as the path, the program type, how to open it, and server commands.

✦ **Main frame caption.** By default, the main window frame's title bar contains the application name. You can change that here. The limit is 28 characters.

✦ **Doc type name.** When you create a new document, the document manager gives it a default name followed by a number. The name defaults to the name of the application, but you can supply a different default here.

✦ **Filter name.** When you open or save a document, the File dialog gives you a list of file types. Each item in the list contains a description of the file type. By default, the description contains the program name followed by the word *Files* and the extension in parentheses. You may override this description in this edit box.

✦ **File new name.** When you have more than one template defined and create a document, a selection dialog appears asking you to select a file type from a list box. The list item is the name you type here.

See also Part III, "Building and Debugging an Application" for steps on adding document templates to your program.

✦ **File type name.** If you selected compound document support in Step 3, type in the name of the file type as you want it to appear in the Windows Registry. By default, it is the application name followed by the word *file*.

Even more Step 4: Window styles

This is the second page of the Advanced Options dialog. If you are creating an SDI application, the bottom portion of this dialog is grayed out. For MDI applications, the following descriptions, except for the system menu, apply to the child windows:

✦ **Thick frame.** Provides a thick border around the frame. Note that if you don't select this option, the user can't resize the window after it is created other than to maximize it.

✦ **Minimize box.** Provides a box (using the "_" symbol) in the upper-right corner of the window to minimize the window

✦ **Maximize box.** Provides a box in the upper-right corner to maximize the window

✦ **System menu.** Provides a drop-down menu when the icon is clicked to minimize, maximize, move, or close the window. With thick frame, the menu also includes options to resize and restore the window to its original size.

✦ **Minimized.** Causes the application to run as an icon on the task bar at the bottom of the desktop (or, for a child window, at the bottom of the main window).

✦ **Maximized.** Causes the application window to fill the entire screen on startup. Child windows fill the client area.

Step 5: Comments and library options

When the wizard generates source code, it places explanatory comments in the code. Many programmers prefer to have the comments, but you can opt out by politely selecting the No, Thank You check box.

You also have the option of using the MFC library as a DLL or by statically linking it to your program. Most programs use a shared library (DLL) because static linking incorporates all the MFC code into your program. That means larger program size and longer startup times.

Note: Static linking is available only in the Professional and Enterprise editions of Visual C++.

Step 6: Naming your classes

Decide here whether to accept the wizard's choice of class names. Select each class name in the window panel, and look at the edit boxes below the panel for the wizard's choices; change them if you don't like the defaults.

Most classes have fixed bases, and therefore, the Base Class window is disabled. Clicking on view class in the window panel enables the Base Class combo box, and you may select a different view class. The table outlines your choice of view classes.

Base Class	Features
CView	The base class for views. Includes only basic support for display and editing of a document's data
CEditView	Contains a standard edit control with support for text editing, searching, replacing, and scrolling
CRichEditView	Contains all the support of CEditView and also includes support for fonts, colors, paragraph formatting, and embedded OLE objects

(continued)

Base Class	Features
CFormView	A scroll view, the basic layout of which you define in a dialog template
CListView	The derived class contains a list control similar to that seen when you open a Windows folder
CScrollView	Base class for views with automatic scrolling capabilities
CTreeView	The derived class contains a tree control, which displays a hierarchical list of icons and labels. The view is similar to the left-hand panel of Windows 95 Explorer

Click the Finish button and look over the application specs. If you don't like what you see, click the Cancel button and go back through the wizard to make changes. Otherwise, click the OK button. The wizard generates a lot of code based upon the options you select.

Project Settings

Normally, the AppWizard sets up two configurations for your program, "Debug" and "Release," but you can add others. You may have a valued customer who wants some specific changes to your program. By setting up a custom build for this customer and including the altered code in conditional statements, you don't have to maintain a completely separate copy of the program. The active configuration may be changed by selecting Build⇨Set Active Configuration. When you're ready to set your program loose on the world, change the configuration to Release (or the build for your valued customer) and rebuild it.

The IDE has a rich set of options you can set for each build, or the setting may be applied to all builds. Select Project⇨Settings or type Alt+F7 to get the settings dialog.

Tab	What You Can Do
General	Modify static/dynamic options. Specify build directories.
Debug page	Set Working directories, insert startup arguments, specify paths for DLLs your program needs.
C/C++	Set warning message, browse, and optimizations. Set language, code and build options.
Link	Specify output and custom library locations.
Resources	Set the name of the compiled resource file to use and any other directories for resource (.res) files. Lets you share .res files between projects.

Tab	What You Can Do
OLE Types	Specify an object description language (.ODL) file.
Browse Info	Set the location of the browse files. If you check the "Build browse info file" box, make sure to select the browser check box on the C++ page.
Custom Build	Specify build commands and files when performing a custom build.
Pre-link Step	Specify commands to run after the creation of the object files but before the linker generates the executable file.
Post-build Step	Commands to execute after the build is complete. This may include creating a compressed file for inclusion on a setup disk.

If you expand the tree on the left and select a source, header, or resource file, you get a different set of options: You can specify files that you don't want to include in the build or object file locations.

Utility Libraries

If you find that you are writing the same functions over and over, you may want to include them in a library file, compile the file once, and then link the compiled functions to your applications as you need them. To build a utility library, follow these steps:

1. Select New from the main menu; then select Win32 Static Library from the New dialog.

You don't need to do any specific coding such as `WinMain()`, `InitInstance()`, or class-creation coding. The wizard adds the necessary compiler commands to create the library for you.

Remember: The application wizard sets up only the project files; you have to create the source files.

2. Add source and header files to the project as you need them.

Note: You may want to place each function in its own source file. Doing so allows you to link each routine as its own module rather than having to link the entire library into your program.

Part III

Building and Debugging a Project

A wise programmer once observed that any program can be shortened by at least one line of code and contains at least one undiscovered bug, from which it follows that any program can be reduced to one line of code that doesn't work. Obviously, you want to write the tightest code possible with the least number of bugs — preferably none. Creating a program is a repetitive process of writing code and testing it. During the writing phase, you create files and classes, add variables and functions, and make your code handle the many Windows messages. Errors are inevitable, but you can clean them up easily. A few examples of debugging methods include breakpoints, stepping through a program, and watches.

In this part . . .

- ✔ Using breakpoints
- ✔ Adding classes
- ✔ Compiling the application
- ✔ Debugging your code
- ✔ Adding member functions
- ✔ Stepping through a program
- ✔ Finding and repairing program errors
- ✔ Setting and using watches
- ✔ Adding Windows Message Handlers

Adding Classes to a Project

If you're adding a new class derived from an MFC class to your project, by far the easiest way is to invoke the ClassWizard. This wizard creates source and header files for you, inserts the class constructors and destructors, declares a message map, and adds some debugging code.

See also "The ClassWizard" in this part for a description of the ClassWizard.

Remember: Generic classes — those not derived from MFC or a type library — can't be added by using the ClassWizard.

Adding an MFC class using the ClassWizard

You can use the ClassWizard only to add classes derived from MFC base classes.

See also "Adding Generic Classes" in this section.

To add a class using the ClassWizard, follow these steps:

1. Invoke the wizard by choosing View⇨ClassWizard or pressing Ctrl+W.

2. Click the Add Class button on the upper right on any tab of the ClassWizard.

3. A popup list (actually a menu) appears. You have two choices: "New" and "From a type library." Select New from the list.

4. In the dialog box that pops up, give the new class a name in the Name edit box. As you type the name of the new class, the wizard builds a default filename for it in the File Name edit box. You can change the filename by clicking the Change button. Yet another dialog box will pop up. Enter the name you want for the header file in the Header File edit box and the program file name in the Implementation File edit box. Use the Browse buttons if you want to include the new class in an existing file.

5. Select a base class from the Base Class combo box. The drop-down list contains the Microsoft Foundation Class base class names. The wizard does not create a generic class.

6. If your new class is for a dialog box, select the resource ID from the list in the Dialog ID combo box.

7. Click the OK button.

To begin working on the new class, click the Edit Code button, and the wizard opens the source file.

Adding a generic class

Use the following steps to add generic classes. You can also use this method to create classes derived from MFC base classes.

1. Summon the generic New Class dialog box by choosing Insert⇨New Class.

2. Choose MFC or Generic in the Class Type box. If you created your project with the ATL COM AppWizard, this box also includes an ATL option.

3. Type your new class name in the Name box. A default source file name builds while you add the name; you may give it a different filename by clicking the Change button and entering a file name in the new dialog box that pops up.

- If this is an MFC class, you have to choose a base class from the combo box. Otherwise, a base class name is optional.

- If this is a generic class, you can optionally insert your own base class. To insert a base class, click the highlighted area under Base Class(es), add the base class name, and then choose Public, Private, or Protected from the As column.

4. Click OK.

See also "Accessing Class Members" in Part VIII for a discussion of the `public`, `private`, and `protected` keywords.

Adding Document Templates

The MFC AppWizard gives you the option of setting up only one template for your application's documents. Eventually, you're going to write an application that needs to handle more than one type of document.

Adding templates, even late in the program development, is a simple task involving two steps. First, you need to create a string table entry to define the template, and then you need to add the code to register the template.

Step 1: Adding a string table entry

To add a string table entry, follow these steps:

1. Select the ResourceView pane in the Workspace window. Click on the plus sign next to String Table to expand the list.

2. Double-click the string table entry in which you want to add the template definition. (You probably can only see one string table entry.) This brings up a dialog box with a list control containing the string table entries.

3. Scroll to the bottom of the list control. You'll find an empty string entry. Double-click it to reveal a String Properties dialog box.

4. In the String Properties dialog box, enter a resource ID for the new string in the ID box. This ID should be something like IDR_RICHTEXTTYPE.

5. In the Caption box, enter the string text using the fields in the table below. Each field is separated by a newline (\n) character; if you omit a field, you still have to have a newline character.

The fields in the following table appear in the order they must be placed in the string.

Field	Explanation
Window title	This field appears in the application window's title bar. It is ignored for MDI applications.
Document name	The root name that will be used when new documents of this type are created. The document manager will append a number to this name. If blank, "Untitled" is used.
FileNew name	The text displayed in the dialog box when the File⇨New command is invoked. The dialog box is displayed only if more than one template exists.
Filter name	The text is displayed in the Files of Type combo box in the File Open dialog box when the File⇨Open command is invoked.
Filter extension	The extension used when displaying files of this type in dialog boxes. If not present, files of this type cannot be accessed through the dialog boxes (such as the File Open dialog box).
Registration ID	Used by the Windows File Manager to register the file type in the database maintained by Windows. If not specified, the file type is not registered.
Registration name	The text displayed in dialog boxes of applications that access the registration database.

The following is an example of what the string would look like for a template for rich text (.rtf) documents:

```
Rich Text\nRichText\nRich Text Documents
(*.rtf)\nRich Text Documents (*.rtf)\n.RTF\nRich
Text Document.1\nRich Text Document
```

The code above displays a window title of "Rich Text," displays a document name of "RichText," displays "Rich Text Documents (*.rtf)" in the New dialog box, and so on. Notice how the \n character separates the fields.

Step 2: Creating and adding a template

After creating a string table entry, you need to create the actual template and call the AddDocTemplate() function. Both of these are done in the InitInstance() function of your application.

You can find the right place to create the template by searching for the commented line // Register the application's document templates.

The following is sample code that defines an .rtf template and calls AddDocTemplate to add it to your application:

```
CMultiDocTemplate* pRtfTemplate;
pRtfTemplate = new CMultiDocTemplate(
    IDR_RICHTEXTTYPE,
    RUNTIME_CLASS(CMyDoc),
    RUNTIME_CLASS(CChildFrame),
    RUNTIME_CLASS(CMyView));
AddDocTemplate(pRtfTemplate);
```

First, this code sets pRtfTemplate as a pointer to a CMultiDocTemplate object, which is the multidocument template interface. (If you're using a single-document interface, substitute CSingleDocTemplate for CMultiDocTemplate.) Then the code creates a new instance of the CMultiDocTemplate that pRtfTemplate refers to. The first parameter is the ID for the particular template. Replace CMyDoc and CMyView with the class names for your document and view classes. Finally, the code calls AddDocTemplate() to add the new .rtf template to your application.

Adding Functions to a Class

Adding functions to a class with the IDE tools can save a lot of time and errors. If you use the dialog boxes accessed through the Wizard Bar down arrow, you can enter the function type and any parameters, and the tool inserts the declaration in your header file and the body of the function in the source file. All you have to do is to add the code in between.

Adding member functions

From time to time, you may need to add your own functions to your class. You can manually add the declaration to your header file and then add the function definition to the source file. The Wizard Bar simplifies this task and reduces the chance of error by making the declaration and definition identical. You still have to do the programming, but the tools handle the grunt work.

To add a member function:

1. Whisk up to the Wizard bar and click the Action button's down arrow.

2. Choose Add Member Function from the pop-up menu. The Add Member Function dialog box appears.

3. Give your function a type in the Function Type edit box. The type may be any of the C++ data types or any type that has been previously defined.

4. In the Function Declaration dialog box, type the function declaration as you would declare it in the header file. Include any data types when entering parameters. Do not include the terminating semicolon. For example,

```
MyFunction(int MyInt, char *MyPointer)
```

5. Select the appropriate check box in the Access group for the security for the function — public, private, or protected.

6. Select the appropriate check box at the bottom of the dialog box to declare whether the function is to be static or virtual.

Click OK. The dialog box closes, and the source file opens with the cursor at the new function's definition.

Using virtual functions

Use a virtual function to override a function of the same name in a base class.

See also "Virtual Functions" in Part VIII for an explanation of virtual functions.

To add a virtual function to your class:

1. Access the Wizard Bar's pop-up menu by clicking on the Action button's down arrow.

2. Select Add Virtual Functions from the list. If your base classes have no virtual functions that may be overridden, a message box tells you so (you can't go any further).

3. In the New Virtual Override dialog box, select the function to add from the New Virtual Functions list box. When you add it, the function moves to the Existing Virtual Function Overrides list box.

> *Note:* If the function already has been added, click the Edit Existing button to go to the source code file.

4. If you're adding more than one virtual function, click the Add Function button. If this is the last or only function, click the Add and Edit button to close the dialog box and go to the source code.

Adding Windows Message Handlers

A Windows program receives a constant stream of messages from the operating system. Almost anything that happens in an application — a mouse movement, a key pressed, a button pushed — generates a message. Your program may opt to ignore the message or handle it with your own code. If you choose to ignore the message, it will be processed by MFC message handlers, if one exists to handle the message.

On a dialog box, for example, the MFC `CDialog` base class has default functions for handling the OK and Cancel buttons, but you may override them with your own code. Your own message handlers need to handle any other buttons you add to the dialog.

You can use two tools to help you add message handlers: the ClassWizard and the Wizard Bar. The ClassWizard is the quicker method for dialog box functions.

Adding a message handler with ClassWizard

Using the ClassWizard makes adding message handlers for dialog box controls easy. If you have the dialog box open, the wizard will locate the resource ID for the control and select it when you summon the wizard.

To add a message handler:

1. Summon the ClassWizard with Ctrl+W or choose View⟿ClassWizard. For a dialog box control, simply right-click the control and select ClassWizard from the pop-up menu that appears.

2. Make sure the Project and Class Name boxes show the class to which you want to add the message handler. The default selects the active window active at the time you invoke the wizard.

3. Click the Message Map tab. You'll see three list boxes: Object IDs, Messages, and Member Functions.

4. Locate the resource ID of the object in the Object IDs list, and select the class name. The Messages list box will contain a list of base class virtual functions followed by a list of messages that currently are not being handled in the base class. The Member Functions list box will contain virtual functions that have been overridden and message handler functions already in your class.

5. Choose the message or handler function name in the Messages list. (A listing in bold indicates a function that already has been overridden or a message for which a handler has already been added.)

Remember: The Member Functions list box just below the Object IDs and Message panels contains message functions already in your class. The V icon indicates a virtual function, and the W icon indicates a Windows message function.

6. Click the Add Function button to add the function to your class. You then may press the Edit Code button to open the source file.

Pressing the Edit Code button instead of the Add Function button first adds the function, closes the ClassWizard dialog box and takes you to the source file in a single step.

7. Exit the ClassWizard by clicking OK.

Adding a message handler with the Wizard Bar

The context-tracking feature of the Wizard Bar makes adding message handlers easy. As you edit program files, the bar keeps track of where you are and is always ready to act on the current class.

To add a message handler using the Wizard Bar:

1. Make sure the Wizard Bar Class Box displays the class in which you want to insert a message handler. If you're editing a source file, the context tracking selects the class you're working on.

2. In the Filter box, choose the resource ID or object you want your new function to handle.

3. Click the Action button. The default action should be Add Windows Message Handler.

To confirm the default action, pause the mouse for a second with the pointer over the Action button. The pop-up tool tip shows you the action the bar will take when you press it.

4. In the New Windows Message and Event Handlers dialog box, the Class or Object to Handle lists should have the Filter box selection highlighted. If not, select it now.

5. The New Windows Messages/Events list box contains the messages that are available for the selected object. Click the one you want to add.

The Existing Message/Event Handlers list box shows message handlers that already are added to your source file. If your handler already is in the source code, click the Edit Existing button. The source file opens with the cursor on the message function.

6. If you want to add multiple message handlers, click the Add Handler button and select the next message. If this is the only or last message handler you want to add now, click the Add and Edit button.

7. If you clicked the Add and Edit button, the dialog box closes and the source file opens. If not, click the Edit Existing button to close the dialog box and open the source file.

You can bypass the first three steps by pressing the Action button's down arrow and selecting Add Windows Message Handler from the pop-up menu. In this case, you have to find and select the class or object to handle yourself.

If the base class already had a message handler for the object (for example, an OK button), the new handler will include a call to it. Whether you add your code before or after the call depends upon the function. You can delete the call and handle the message entirely yourself.

Breakpoints

Breakpoints allow you to pause execution of a program when they are encountered. You can place conditions on a breakpoint, and the program will halt only when the conditions you specify are true.

A breakpoint without conditions is handy when you know the approximate location of a program bug. You can set the breakpoint near that point and then inspect variables as you single-step through the suspect code.

See also "Stepping through a Program" in this Part.

Setting breakpoints

Set a breakpoint by locating the statement in the source file where you want the break to occur. Press the Insert/Remove Breakpoint button on the Build toolbar, or press F9.

See also "Conditional breakpoints" in this part if you want the breakpoint to halt the program only under certain conditions.

Clearing breakpoints

You can clear a breakpoint two ways: Use the Breakpoints dialog box, or find the breakpoint in your code and manually clear it.

To clear a breakpoint using the dialog box:

1. Choose Edit⇨Breakpoints, or press Alt+F9.

2. Locate the breakpoint in the Breakpoints list box at the bottom of the dialog box. To disable and enable the breakpoint without deleting it, toggle the check mark you see in the box just to the left of the breakpoint ID.

3. To remove the breakpoint completely, select it, and then press the Delete key. To clear all the breakpoints, click the Remove All button.

To clear a breakpoint in the source code file:

1. Open the file containing the breakpoint.

2. Scroll through the file until you find the breakpoint. Each breakpoint has a red dot to the left of the statement.

3. Click the Insert/Remove Breakpoint button on the Build toolbar, or press F9.

Conditional breakpoints

To set a conditional breakpoint, you must first set a breakpoint and then perform the following steps:

See also "Setting breakpoints" in this part.

1. Choose Edit⇨Breakpoints.

2. In the Breakpoints dialog box, select the breakpoint in the list box at the bottom.

3. Click the Condition button to display the Breakpoint Condition dialog box.

4. Type the condition that must be true for the breakpoint to execute. The condition should be a valid C++ expression that evaluates to true or false.

For example, type **i == 3** instead of **i = 3**.

5. In the box at the bottom of the dialog box, type the number of times to skip the breakpoint before stopping the program. Leave the box blank to stop the program every time the condition is true.

6. Click OK to close the Condition dialog box, and then click OK to close the Breakpoints dialog box.

Building an Application

Building refers to the entire process of compiling individual source files and linking them together into a program.

Visual C++ builds two versions of your program. The first version is the Debug version, which contains information the debugger needs to step through your program. The second version is the Release version, which is fully optimized. The executable file is larger in the Debug version than in the Release version, which means it takes more disk space and needs more time to load itself into memory.

The first step in building is compiling the files. You can spend a lot of time writing C++ code, but none of it is useful to your computer. C++ code must be turned (compiled) into machine code — object code — for the computer. Think of compiling as akin to translating a book. You can read source code, but the computer can't. Likewise, the computer can read object code, but you can't. The compiler is the translator.

After your program compiles, the source code turns into object files, one for each source file. The object files can't run by themselves, so the IDE invokes a linker to put them together into a single, executable program file.

Building a Debug version

You use the Debug version of your program during its development. The Debug version contains symbolic information such as line numbers and variable names so that the debugger can trace the execution of your program.

If you have browsing enabled, the browser files (the .sbr files) are created in the Debug version.

To see which version you're using when you click the Build button, choose Build⇨Set Active Configuration. The Set Active Project Configuration dialog box highlights the current configuration. You can change the version in this dialog box. To compile a Debug version of your application, make sure you select the Win32 Debug version. You can start the compilation three ways:

  ✦ Choose Build⇨Build MyApp.exe (or whatever your program executable is called).

  ✦ Press F7.

✦ Press the Build button on the Build toolbar or the Build MiniBar, whichever you have displayed (usually the minibar).

In each case, the Output Window tab switches to Build, and Visual C++ displays the progress of the compile (including any errors or warnings encountered).

If you get an error or warning message, double-click on the line in the Output Window. The source file opens with the cursor at the offending location.

A warning message doesn't stop your program from running, and sometimes it's difficult or impossible to avoid a warning. Check warnings out because they may indicate some construct that can cause unexpected program errors.

Building a Release version

When you're satisfied your program works the way you want, you can build a release version to give to others. You will want to use this version as well, because it's smaller and runs faster than the Debug version.

To build the Release version, follow these steps:

1. Choose Build⇨Set Active Configuration.

2. Select the active configuration in the dialog box to Win32 Release, and press OK.

You can start the compilation in one of three ways:

✦ Choose Build⇨Build MyApp.exe (the menu item has the name of your executable file).

✦ Press F7.

✦ Click the Build button on the Build toolbar or the Build MiniBar, whichever you have displayed (usually the minibar).

The Output Window tab switches to Build, and Visual C++ displays the progress of the compilation, including any errors or warnings encountered.

Ideally, your Release build comes up with 0 warnings and 0 errors. Sometimes warnings are unavoidable, but if you have any errors, you have to go back to the Debug version and work them out.

Thoroughly testing your Release version is a good idea. The Release version is optimized, meaning that loops and code may have been consolidated to speed up execution or cut down on program size, but Debug versions usually aren't optimized. Compilers, linkers, and CPUs are better than they used to be; however, in the past, optimization occasionally affected how the program ran.

The ClassWizard

If you've done much C++ programming, you'll really like the ClassWizard shown in the figure below. This wizard is one of the good guys, because it speeds up your programming. The wizard helps you to set up message handlers and member variables. How many times have you added a function or message handler and forgotten to declare it in the header file? Or declared it as the wrong type? Or forgotten to add the class name to the definition? Or any of a number of other errors?

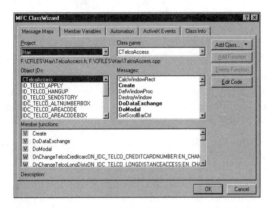

You don't need to worry about any of these details when you use the ClassWizard. You just tell the wizard the function name and type, the parameters and types to use, and how to secure the function. The wizard puts all that information in the header file and creates a function for you in the source file. The wizard even adds a call to the base class function of virtual function overrides.

The ClassWizard and the Wizard Bar are like the Lone Ranger and Tonto. They're a team, and they work well together. While you're figuring out how to use the ClassWizard, check out the Wizard Bar in this part.

Summon the ClassWizard by choosing <u>V</u>iew⇨ClassWizard or by pressing Ctrl+W. The dialog box contains five tabs.

✦ **Message Maps.** Use this tab to set up message handler functions in your class. The list boxes show you resource IDs, virtual functions, and unhandled messages and functions that already have been added to the class.

See also "Wizard Bar" for adding other functions to the class.

✦ **Member Variables.** If the wizard can identify member variables, such as for dialog box objects, a list of their control IDs appears in the Object IDs list. Select the control ID for which you want to add a variable, and click Add Variable. By convention, class variable names begin with "m_", but they don't have to. The wizard selects the category and variable types based on the object, but you can change them here.

✦ **Automation.** If your class supports automation (for example, your document class if you selected automation support when you ran the AppWizard), the Add Method and Add Property buttons are enabled. If these buttons aren't enabled, your class doesn't support automation. Automation allows external programs access to functions in your program. For example, if you're writing a sound editor, you may want other programs to access code in your program to play your files automatically.

✦ **ActiveX Events.** Click Add Event to add an automation event to your code. ActiveX is beyond the scope of this book, and I would recommend additional reading, such as *ActiveX Controls Inside Out* by Adam Denning, published by Microsoft Press.

✦ **Class Info.** This tab lists information about the class that will be built. The Message filter combo box allows you to change the filter in effect. Filters are categorized by type of window or dialog box they operate on. Foreign Class and Foreign Variable allow you to insert a pointer variable to an object of this class into your application.

All tabs in the ClassWizard have two combo boxes in common. The Project and Class Name combo boxes appear at the top of each page. Use them to choose the project (in most cases you have only one project available) and the class you want to work with.

Each page also has an Add Class button, which you can use to create classes derived from MFC or from a type library. You cannot create generic classes with this control.

See also "Adding Classes to a Project" for steps to create new classes.

Compiling a Single File

The wizards of Visual C++ may be perfect programmers, but the rest of us aren't. As you build your code, errors can creep in. Test-compile your code from time to time to keep it clean.

A single error can create a long stream of error messages, and if you have added a lot of code between compiles, you have to sift through a lot to find the problem spot.

Also, a missing brace, either { or }, can go undetected by the compiler for many lines. In addition, the line where it actually generates an error can be 20 or 30 lines later in the program. If you've added only a few lines between test compiles, you know where to look for the error.

Compiling a single file doesn't generate a new program file; it only builds the object file for the single module. To test-run your program, you have to go through a complete build.

To compile a single file:

1. Select the source file (.cpp) in the editor window. You can't compile a header (.h) file.

2. Use one of the following three methods to start the compiler:

• Choose Build➪Compile <filename>.

• Press Ctrl+F7.

• Click the Compile button on the Build toolbar or the Build minibar.

3. The output window at the bottom switches to the Build tab. Keep an eye on it for errors and warnings.

4. To stop the compile, click the Stop Build button on the Build toolbar or press Ctrl+Break. A Stop Build item also gets added to the menu.

See also "Building a Debug version" in this part for steps to create a trial executable program.

Debugging

Like it or not, at some time during your programming a mistake will creep in and you'll face the task of finding and fixing it. No matter how much experience you have, you still may manage to write code that doesn't work or doesn't perform the way you want.

Finding those problem spots is the job of the debugger.

Assuming you built the debug version of your project, to start it running in the debugger, choose Build➪Start Debug➪Go, press F5, or click the Go button on the Build toolbar.

See also "Building an Application" in this Part for steps on building the debug version of your program.

A lot of debugging technique is intuition and experience. Generally, you will know the approximate location of the bug from writing the program. Set a breakpoint in the code, and run your program until it encounters the breakpoint. Step through the code until you find the line or function causing the bug.

See also "Stepping through a Program" in this part for details on using the single-step functions of the debugger and "Breakpoints" for setting and using breakpoints.

During debugging, you can pause execution at any point by pressing the Break Execution button on the Debug toolbar.

If you still can't locate the area of the bug, you can use what I call the *work-your-way-down technique.*

1. Set the cursor at a point in the code *before* the bug occurs.

2. Choose Build⊏⊃Start Debug⊏⊃Run to Cursor, or press Ctrl+F10.

3. Use the Step Over button on the Debug tool bar (or F10) to step over each function call in your code.

4. When the bug occurs, the function that was being executed is the culprit. Stop the program, reset the cursor at this point, and rerun it. This time, *step into* the function you know caused the bug, and single-step until you find it.

The bug may be several function calls deep, but you can repeat this process until you work your way down to the function that is causing the problem. Single-step the code using the Step Into or Step Over buttons until the bug occurs.

Editing Program Files

The IDE contains a multiple-document client window that makes it possible to have multiple files open at the same time.

When you create a project, the wizards don't open any files for you. The IDE provides a number of ways you can open files, however.

✦ Choose File⊏⊃Open, or type Ctrl+O. Select the file from the Open dialog box.

✦ In the File View pane of the Workspace Window, expand the tree for the type file you want to open. Double-click on the file name to open it.

✦ In the Class View menu of the Workspace Window, double-click on a class name to open the file that contains the definition of the class. Usually this is a header (.h) file. Expand the class name and double-click on a member function to open the source file (usually .cpp) that contains the body of the function. The cursor appears at the function definition.

+ In the Resource View menu of the Workspace Window, double-click on a resource object to open the resource file and start the resource editor for that object.

+ Use the Wizard Bar to navigate to a function or class definition. The header or source file opens with the cursor placed on the object.

Unless you change the default configuration, the IDE saves any changed files when you build your project. When you close a project, you receive a prompt to save each file that has changed.

The editor maintains an undo buffer of 65,536 operations. According to the Help file, the Windows 95 Registry sets the size, and I haven't found any way to modify it other than to edit the registry entry.

After you undo an operation, you can still change your mind and click the Redo button.

Error Handling

The best way to keep your program running smoothly is to compile often. Write a few lines of code and compile; that way, you know within a few lines where to find any errors. You don't have to run your program with every compile, although test-driving the code often to find and eliminate any programming errors is a good idea.

Programming errors

Programming errors include logic problems, failure to initialize a variable, invalid pointers, and so on. The preprocessors in the compiler are good at sniffing out a number of common programming errors; however, a number of errors are perfectly good programming constructs but just don't work.

Consider the following classic program error. Although the code doesn't do much, it's still perfectly good code and the compiler doesn't even issue a warning. Modern PCs should take only a few microseconds to execute it; but when you run the program, it comes to a grinding halt.

```
i = 4;
while (i);
{
    --i;
}
```

Even experienced programmers generate this bug from time to time. You are so used to putting a semicolon at the end of each statement that the error may escape you even after scanning the code several times. Fix the bug by removing the semicolon after the while statement.

The only way to find these errors is by careful examination of the code or single-stepping through the program.

See also "Debugging" in this section for a technique for finding tips on bugs.

Syntax errors

Syntax errors derive from code the compiler can't understand. Such an error may be something as simple as a missing semicolon, a variable or class name used improperly or missing, or an extra brace, such as { or }. The missing brace error is particularly insidious, because the compiler may not flag the error until several lines later in the code, when it finally gets so confused it figures there must be an error.

Usually, with syntax errors, the compiler error messages give a clue on how to fix the mistake, but sometimes you have to read the messages carefully.

Don't be discouraged if a compile generates numerous errors, particularly if you've just typed a few lines of code. Sometimes a simple declaration error can produce 50 or 60 errors. Just go to the top of the list, and go through the errors; often you find many of the errors are related and produced by the same line of code.

Exception Handling

Your program may be bug-free (my, aren't you the dreamer), but it still may encounter errors that you can't control. Reading or writing a file to disk, for example, may generate an unexpected error. These errors are called *exceptions,* and they can be serious in the Release version of your program.

Fortunately, the C++ language specifies procedures to deal with exceptions. Microsoft handles them a little differently in Visual C++, but the result is that with exception handling, your code doesn't have to keep checking for unexpected errors. When an error occurs, you can catch it, deal with it, and resume your program.

MFC has several exception classes.

Exception	Meaning
CFileException	Designates an error encountered during a file operation. The file may not be open, the disk may be full or write-protected.
CArchiveException	Shows an error similar to a file exception except it's thrown during serialization.
CMemoryException	Memory error, usually out of memory. The new operators throw this exception automatically. If you use the old malloc statement, you need to detect the error (malloc returns a NULL on error) and throw the exception yourself.
CSimpleException	Thrown when the program makes a request for a feature that isn't available.
CResourceException	Thrown when Windows cannot find or allocate memory for a requested resource.
CUserException	Used when the user performs some unexpected operation that interferes with normal processing. Usually used with a message box to alert the user.
COleException	Thrown when an error occurs during an OLE operation.
CDaoException	Indicates an error during an operation on a Data Access Object.
CDBException	Indicates an error during execution of an Open Database Class operation.
COleDispatchException	Thrown when an error occurs during an automation operation.

The class library functions throw most of these exceptions when they detect an error. You are responsible for catching and processing the error without interrupting your program flow. If you don't, then a message box advising the user of an Unhandled Exception appears. The message box usually gives the user the option of stopping the program abruptly, something you don't want to happen if you're in the middle of writing a file.

Don't expect the class library to be aware of every possible user problem that can occur. It's your program; you know what the user should be doing. Generally, you are responsible for throwing *and* catching the CUserException.

The try statement

The try statement sets up a protected block of code. When an exception occurs in this block, it is *thrown,* meaning it is tossed into the air to be caught by an exception handler. If it isn't caught, then it becomes an *unhandled exception.*

The following code depicts a try statement:

```
Try
{
    // Program code that might be subject to an
    // exception being thrown.
}
```

The catch statement

The catch block contains the code to handle a thrown exception, hopefully in a more graceful manner than the operating system would. You can catch an exception, make adjustments in your program and data, and keep the program running.

Catch blocks may be made to intercept particular exceptions, or you can set up a generic catch block. If you're reading a file and allocating memory for the data that is being read in a loop, you may want to handle a file exception differently than a memory exception.

The syntax for the catch statement is `catch (exceptionObject* exceptionName)`. You replace the exceptionObject parameter with one of the Visual C++ exception types. In place of `exceptionName`, enter the variable name that will hold the exception for use in your code.

The following code is a skeleton of how a try-catch block looks:

```
Try
{
    for (I = 0; I < NUMRECORDS; ++I)
    {
        // Allocate memory for a record
        // Read a record into memory
    }
}
catch (CFileException* fe)
{
    // Code to handle the file exception.
}
catch (CMemoryException* me)
{
    // Code to handle the memory exception.
}
```

The preceding code handles only memory and file exceptions. If you want to catch and process any other exception, you can add a generic catch block.

```
catch (CException* e)
{
    // Code to handle any other exceptions.
}
```

```
// Normal program code following
// the catch blocks.
```

The generic exception handler must be the last catch block in the sequence.

Searching for Text

Visual C++ provides a number of powerful search mechanisms. The familiar `grep` command is missing from the IDE Tools menu. In its place, you find edit boxes for entering regular expressions. (The `grep` command took its name from the phrase "get regular expression.") Until you get used to it, writing regular expressions for `grep` can take more looking up the syntax in the manual than searching through the text yourself. The Visual C++ search dialog boxes have some tools that make it easy.

Bookmarks

Bookmarks allow you to save the location in a file and return to it later. Visual C++ provides two types of bookmarks: ordinary and named.

An *ordinary bookmark* indicates only the line that is marked. This bookmark is temporary and is lost when the file closes or reloads. You recognize an ordinary bookmark by a cyan (sort of light blue) box in the left margin.

To set or clear an ordinary bookmark:

1. Locate the line you want to mark, and place the cursor on it.

2. Toggle the bookmark using the Toggle Bookmark tool in the Edit toolbar, or press Ctrl+F2.

3. To turn off the bookmark, repeat these steps.

Visual C++ retains named bookmarks when the file — or even the IDE itself — closes. You may return to the named bookmark anytime, even in successive programming sessions.

To set a named bookmark:

1. Place the cursor at the location of the word or text you want to mark.

2. Summon the Bookmark dialog box by choosing Edit↔ Bookmarks or pressing Alt+F2.

3. In the Name box, type the name you want to give the bookmark.

4. Click the Add button, or press Enter. The bookmark gets added to the list.

In stepping from one bookmark to the next (or previous), named bookmarks are visited in order with ordinary bookmarks. Use the Next Bookmark (F2) and Previous Bookmark (Shift+F2) tools in the Edit toolbar.

You can also jump directly to a named bookmark:

1. Choose Edit⇨Bookmarks.

2. Choose the bookmark from the list (the filename and line number appear at the bottom of the dialog box).

3. Click the Go To button.

To clear ordinary bookmarks, press the Clear All Bookmarks tool or press Ctrl+Shift+F2. You can clear named bookmarks in the dialog box by choosing them and then clicking Delete.

The Find command

Select Edit⇨Find or press Ctrl+F to summon the Find dialog box. The box for entering your search string is a combo box that stores up to 16 of your previous searches. In addition, at the end of the box, you see an arrow pointing to the right. The arrow takes you to the regular expression tool.

Option	*Meaning*
Match Whole Word Only	The searches are matched only if they are preceded and followed by white space or punctuation, or if they fall at the beginning or end of a line.
Match Case	The case characters in the string must match the case of the characters in the Find What box.
Regular Expression	The contents of the Find What box are used as a regular expression for searching.
Search All Open Documents	Searches for the string in all files open in the workspace. If you need to search all files, open or not, use the Find in Files command.
Up/Down radio buttons	Chooses whether to search forward or backward through the text.
Find Next button	Searches through the text stopping at each occurrence of the search string.
Mark All button	Searches through the entire text and places bookmarks at each line that contains a match. You can use the bookmark tools on the Edit toolbar to step through the marked lines.
Regular Expression menu	Summon this menu by pressing the arrow next to the Find Next button. Enter a regular expression item by choosing it in the menu. The Regular Expression check box gets marked automatically.

The Find in Files command and window

Somebody at Microsoft let his imagination run amok when he designed this tool. The result is a super-powerful tool for searching through your source files, whether you have them open in the edit window or not. Visual C++ doesn't have the familiar grep command. The search mechanisms in Visual C++ do provide some grep-like capabilities.

The Find in Files command writes to two panels in the Output Window. You may save the results of two separate searches by choosing alternate panels.

Access the Find in Files dialog box shown in the figure below by selecting File⇨Find In Files or by pressing the Find in Files button on the Standard toolbar.

The dialog box has three combo boxes plus several options that let you search through multiple directories and restrict your search. To use the Find in Files command:

1. Type the text you want to search for in the Find What box. The IDE saves up to 16 of your previous searches, and you can choose one by pressing the down arrow on the combo box. Pressing the right-pointing arrow just to the right of this box brings up a menu of grep-like search patterns. The syntax is not the same as grep, but they serve the same purpose.

2. In the In Files/File Types box, choose the filter for the type of files you want to search through. Select *.* to search all files.

3. Select the directory to search through using the In Folder combo box. Using this and the Advanced button and the Look in Subfolders check box, you can search through multiple directories. Clicking the button (marked with a ".") to the right of this combo box brings up a Choose Directory dialog box.

4. Select the Match Whole Word Only check box to restrict your search to whole words (strings that begin and end with a white space or punctuation marks or that fall at the beginning or end of a line).

5. Select the Match Case check box to limit the found list to either uppercase or lowercase. The case in the search exactly matches the case in the search pattern.

6. To use a grep-like expression, select the Regular Expression check box. If you select an item from the Regular Expression menu, this box is selected automatically.

7. To search through subdirectories of the directory, select the Look in Subfolders check box.

8. Select the Output to Pane 2 check box to output the results in the Find in Files 2 pane of the Output Window. If this check box isn't selected, Visual C++ writes the output to the Find in Files 1 pane.

You can complete most searches by using a combination of these steps. If you need more search options, press the Advanced button.

9. If your project spans multiple directories, you can select the Look in Folders for Project Source Files check box to search them.

10. Select the Look in Folders for Project Include Files check box to extend the search to directories in the include path.

11. To include other directories in the search, type them in the Look in Additional Folders list box. A mini toolbar at the top of this box has tools for entering, deleting, and stepping through entries. If you select the tool to enter a new folder, a button marked with an ellipsis (. . .) appears to the right of the edit line. Click this button to get the Choose Directory dialog box.

12. Click the Find button to conduct the search. The results are listed in one of the Find in Files panels of the Output Window. To go to a line containing the search pattern, double-click the line in the Output Window.

Replacing text

Choose File⇨Replace or type Ctrl+H to display the Replace dialog box. This dialog box is almost guaranteed to produce some head-scratching.

To use the Replace dialog box:

1. In the Find What field, type the string you want to find.

2. In the Replace With field, type the replacement string.

3. Select the Whole Word Only check box to limit the search to words. (A word is a string preceded and followed by white space or punctuation marks or which falls at the beginning or end of a line.)

4. Select the Match Case check box to search only for text matching the case of the text in the Find What field.

5. Select Regular Expression to use grep-like search syntax. The button to the right of the Find What box displays a menu of regular expressions to insert into the box.

6. In the Replace In group, you have two choices.

- If you have an area of a file selected, you can select the Selection radio button to limit the search and replace operation to that block of text.

- Select the Whole File radio button to search the entire file for the Find What string.

7. Alternately click the Find Next and Replace buttons to search for and replace the text. To replace all occurrences of the Find Next string, click the Replace All button.

Stepping through a Program

Like the living variety, bugs can find some clever hiding places. Just looking at the program code won't flush them out, and you have to resort to running the program and examining each line of code. Visual C++ lets you run the program one line at a time, giving you time to examine the results of each line of code.

Stepping into a function

Together with the Step Over button, the Step Into command lets you walk through a program one line at a time. If you press the Step Into button when the program is paused or at a breakpoint on a line containing a function call, then the debugger stops at the first line of the function. If you haven't started the program in the debugger yet, the Step Into command initiates the program and stops at the first line of the code. You can step into the MFC source code, but it's easy to get several layers deep quickly and lose track of the program.

The keyboard command to step into a function call is F11.

Stepping over a function

When you're fairly sure a function is operating properly (or you don't want to step into the MFC source code), you can bypass it by using the Step Over command. The compiler executes the function and stops at the first line after the function call.

Execute the Step Over command by pressing F10.

Stepping out of a function

The Step Out command is handy when you want to get out of a function call (for example, if you accidentally press Step Into when you want Step Over). The Step Out command completes the execution of a function and stops at the first program line after the function call.

Execute the Step Out command by pressing Shift+F11.

Watches

When you start the debugger, the Watch window opens in the lower-right corner of the screen. Watches allow you to keep track of the values of variables or expressions while the program debugs. The watches update only as you step through a program. The Watch window is a tree view, and you can watch the contents of entire structures or classes by clicking on the plus sign next to the name.

The watch window has four tabs, allowing you to keep track of the variables in multiple functions without having to sift through the list.

Setting watches

To add a variable or expression to the watch window:

1. Click on a blank line in the Name column of the Watch window.

2. Type the name of the variable, object, or expression you want to watch.

3. Press Enter.

Clearing watches

To clear or delete a watch, select it in the watch window and press the Delete key.

Using QuickWatch

QuickWatch is an easy way to quickly check the value of a variable or expression without adding it to the watch list. To use the QuickWatch window:

1. Select the window by choosing Tools⇨QuickWatch, or by pressing Shift+F9.

2. Type the name of the variable or expression in the edit box. If you already had used the variable or expression in a QuickWatch, you can select it by pulling down the combo box list.

3. Click Recalculate.

The variable (or all variables in an expression) should be *in scope,* meaning the variables must be accessible from the function or subfunction currently executing. You can't, for example, do a QuickWatch on an automatic variable in the next function.

Wizard Bar

Microsoft deserves a real pat on the back for adding a tool such as the Wizard Bar to the IDE. The other tools aside, the Wizard Bar is super fast. Think of it as a wormhole to various parts of your application; you start at the bar, select your destination, and zip right to it.

You can use the Wizard Bar to add new classes and functions or jump to existing classes and functions. The Wizard Bar uses *context tracking,* which means *it* watches *you* and tries to decide what to put in its selection boxes so that when you're ready to use the Wizard Bar, it's ready to help.

If the Wizard Bar isn't visible on your screen, right-click any empty area on the frame and select it from the pop-up list. The following figure shows the Wizard Bar.

The following list summarizes the controls on the Wizard Bar:

✦ **Class List.** The first combo box on the bar displays classes in the active project. As you select different source files or move the edit cursor from class to class, the name of the class selected in the combo box will change according to where you have the cursor in the source file. If you select a window that has no class, the display is grayed out. For navigation, you may select any class in your project from this box.

✦ **C++ Filters.** This lists the filter for the class displayed in the Class List box. (The filter is used to sort out specific resource IDs.) In this combo box you can select All Class Members, which will list all member functions in the next box, or a specific resource ID.

✦ **Members List.** What appears in the third combo box depends on what you select in the C++ Filters box.

  • If you select All Class Members, this box lists all the member functions of the current class. You can select one of them for navigation.

  • If you select a specific resource ID, this box lists the available message handlers available for the ID. If you select a handler that hasn't been added, the New Windows Message and Event Handlers dialog box appears, which allows you to add the new handler.

✦ **Action button.** This is a two-part button. The left side is like a tool button. Pressing it performs the default Wizard Bar action. To find out what that action is, move the mouse cursor over it for a second and the toolbar tip will tell you. The right side is a down arrow, which you use to call the Action Menu. The following table summarizes the menu items.

Menu Selection	*Action*
Go to Function Declaration	Goes to the source line where the function is declared. Opens the source file if necessary
Go to Function Definition	Goes to the body of the function. Opens the source file if necessary
Add Windows Message Handler	Summons the dialog box to add a message handler
Add Virtual Function	Starts the dialog box to add a function that overrides a base class function
Add Member Function	Opens a dialog box to insert a function into the class
Go to Class Definition	Opens the source code file (if necessary) and positions the cursor at the line where the selected class is defined
New Class	Starts the New Class dialog box for MFC or generic classes
Go to Next Function	Moves the cursor to the next function in the source file
Go to Previous Function	Moves the cursor to the previous function in the source file
Open Include File	Starts a dialog box to select and open any file that is included (with the #include directive) in the file containing the selected class

Part IV

The Resource Workshop

Resources — menus, dialog boxes, toolbars, and so on — are how the user interacts with the program you write. Good design and use of resources can make the difference between a program that is a dreaded chore and one that is easy to use. The Resource Workshop, a part of the Developers Studio, is a powerful and flexible tool. I gloss over or pass some of the older or simpler controls and get into more detail on the newer and more interesting controls, such as the list, animation, and tree controls, along with property sheets and wizards.

In this part . . .

- ✔ Using accelerators
- ✔ Working with bitmaps
- ✔ Using the Common Controls Library
- ✔ Building dialog boxes
- ✔ Finding out about property sheets
- ✔ Making wizards

Accelerators

An accelerator supercharges the keyboard for your program, enabling users to perform menu operations with keystrokes rather than having to maneuver through the menu system.

The MFC AppWizard created a default accelerator table for you with a resource ID of IDR_MAINFRAME. The table loads when you start your application. Edit this table for your application.

Creating and editing accelerators

You can add to the wizard-generated accelerator tables or create your own tables. First, open the accelerator table as follows:

1. Select ResourceView in the Workspace window.

2. Click the + symbol next to Accelerator to display the tables in your project.

3. Highlight the table you want to modify, and open it by double-clicking or pressing return. A panel opens that lists the accelerator keys in the selected table.

To edit an existing accelerator, double-click the line containing the key you want to edit.

To create an accelerator key, double-click the empty rectangle at the bottom of the list. When the Properties box appears, give your new accelerator an ID.

Assigning accelerator IDs

Each accelerator key must have an ID. When you press the key, Windows uses the ID in a command message to your application. If you enter a resource symbol that does not already exist, the workshop assigns it a value and adds it to the resource header file. Generally, accelerator IDs are the same as menu or tool IDs, but they don't have to be. You can have accelerators that do not match menu items, but their IDs must be unique.

Setting accelerator keys

The Key combo box, along with the selection boxes to the right of it, identifies the key that generates the accelerator action. The key can be a typewriter key, a function key, or a keypad stroke.

To enter a base key as the accelerator, just type the character. Preceding the key with a caret (^) creates a control key accelerator. Optionally, you can type the number value of the key in this field and the editor checks the appropriate boxes.

If you enter a value, it must be two or more digits; a single digit is interpreted as the number key itself. To enter a Ctrl+C, for example, make it 03. Be sure you check off the ASCII radio button.

Another way to enter the accelerator is to click the Next Key Typed button. The resource editor reads all the keys that you are pressing (Shift, Alt, or Ctrl) as you strike the next key and select the appropriate check boxes for you.

Make sure the check boxes and the radio buttons to the right have the correct combination for the key you want. You may select among Ctrl, Alt, Shift, any combination of these, or none. Each key, therefore, has eight possible combinations. Shift+Alt+F1, for example, can be assigned a different identifier than Alt+F1.

When you press the Enter key, the accelerator appears on your list.

Creating new accelerator tables

Create new accelerator tables by copying an existing table or by starting from scratch. To create a new table, follow these steps:

1. In the ResourceView, right-click Accelerator.

2. From the popup menu, select Insert Accelerator.

This popup menu is the same for all resource types, but the third item is context-sensitive. In this case, it shows Insert Accelerator because you clicked Accelerator.

3. Give the table a distinctive name and go through the process of creating and editing new accelerators to build the new table as described in the "Setting accelerator keys" section.

Animation Controls

Most users are introduced to animation when they first install Windows 95. Remember that snare drum on the setup wizard? If you bought a machine with Windows 95 already installed, you missed it, but you can see another example of it when you use the drag-and-drop method of copying files. The little sheet of paper flying through the air from one folder to another is an animation control.

You can create buttons to display animations when clicked. The control can play only AVI files that have no sound. The only compression allowed is Run-Length Encoding (RLE); otherwise, the .avi file must not be compressed. Coming up with a .avi file is pretty easy; making it meet those restrictions is a bit more difficult. I haven't seen a bitmap editor that can handle .avi files very well. But, then, I haven't really looked for one. If you're looking for a good project for your new Visual C++, how about an AVI editor? The samples directory of the CD has a nifty animated cursor that looks as though it may be modified to edit animation files. Also, you can find lots of information on the AVI file format on the Internet and in the Visual C++ header files.

You can get that file copy animation file — plus the little moving flashlight used in the network neighborhood and a little jumping armadillo — by retrieving the CMNCTRLS demonstration program. Just follow these steps:

1. In the InfoViewer search panel, type **common controls, sample programs.** You get a topic called Common Control Sample List. Open it.

2. Select the CMNCTRLS sample program.

3. Click Copy All, and specify the directory.

4. When all the files are copied, close the dialog box and open the workspace in the directory where you copied the files.

The CMNCTRLS sample program is a nifty little dialog-based program that demonstrates several of the Windows 9*x* controls. Look in the directory you copied it to and you'll find three animation files: dillo.avi, filecopy.avi, and search.avi. Use these files to experiment with the animation control. While you're at it, you may go ahead and compile the CMNCTRLS program; it's informative and entertaining.

To use the animation control:

1. Create an animation control on your dialog. What you see isn't very exciting. In fact, if you don't put a border or a frame edge on it, the control sinks into the dialog background. Turn off the grid lines and you can't even tell it's there, but that's the idea of the animation control. If you're planning to use filecopy.avi, make the control wide.

2. Add a variable for your control in your dialog box's header file, something like

```
CAnimateCtrl  m_animate;
```

Do not use the ClassWizard to add this variable. The wizard adds it to the `DoDataExchange` function, which guarantees an exception when you run it. If you use the wizard, be sure to delete the `DDX` item.

3. You can use a program event to trigger an animation.

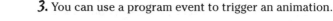

To start the animation, add the following code:

```
const char *filename =
  "E:\\CFILES\\COMNCTRL\\filecopy.avi";
// Or wherever you placed the file
  m_animate.Stop ();
  m_animate.Close ();
  int result = m_animate.Open (filename);
  if (result)
  m_animate.Play(0, -1, -1);
```

This code stops and closes any previous incarnation of the control and then opens the file and plays it. In Play(), 0 means to start with the first frame and -1 to play through to the end of the file; the final -1 parameter makes it repeat until stopped. The CAnimateCtrl class doesn't have a lot of member functions, and most of them appear in the snippet of code. The only other member function is Seek(UINT frame) to display a single frame of the .avi file. You may also need the Create() function if the control isn't placed on a dialog.

Bitmaps

A bitmap is a collection of bits that describe the image as it would appear on the screen or on a printer. In the case of color bitmaps, the bits also contain color information. Bitmaps can be used to illustrate menus, buttons, or dialog boxes.

The graphics editor in the Resource Workshop isn't very good for handling large or higher-resolution graphics (bitmaps can't really be called *high* resolution graphics), but the editor is acceptable for drawing icons, cursors, and the small bitmaps that fit on buttons. If you plan to use larger bitmaps in your program, you may want to look into programs such as Paint Shop Pro, which have much greater abilities to draw, manipulate, and resize images. You can import the bitmap output of other graphics programs into the Workshop very easily.

See also "Importing bitmaps" in this part.

Creating and editing bitmaps

The MFC AppWizard does not create any bitmap objects when you create a project. To create a bitmap, follow these steps:

1. Right-click on any item in the Resource View of the Workspace Window.

2. Select Insert from the popup menu.

3. From the resource tree control, choose Bitmap, and then click New.

The default frame is a drawing window that is 48 pixels square, the size of a large icon. For anything larger than this, you'll have to create the graphic with a good graphics editor, save the result as a bitmap, and then import it into the workshop as described in the following section.

Importing bitmaps

Importing bitmaps for use in your program is the only good reason for invoking the bitmap editor. The workshop editor can only crop, rotate, and flip the image. This editor also has some capabilities for adjusting colors, but doing so is much easier to do in other graphic editing editors.

1. Using an editor such as Paint Shop Pro, draw or edit your image. Save the image in the external editor as a Windows RLE Encoded bitmap.

Make sure the resulting image is the size you want; you cannot resize bitmaps in the workshop.

2. Return to the Workshop, and right-click on any item in the Resource View.

3. Select Insert from the popup menu.

4. Select Bitmap from the Resource Type list, and then click the Import button. The Import Resource dialog box appears.

5. Select the .bmp file containing the image you saved in the other editor.

6. When the image appears, deselect the Save Compressed check box.

The file is already compressed. If you leave the Save Compressed check box selected, the bitmap editor tries to compress it again, giving you some strange results.

At this point, you can make only simple changes to the bitmap image. You can rotate the image through multiples of 90 degrees or flip it horizontally or vertically using the main menu. You can also crop the image, but any major editing at this point is not a good idea because of the limited capabilities of the bitmap editor.

Creating toolbars from bitmaps

The most interesting and useful feature of the bitmap object is the editor's ability to convert any bitmap, even scanned images, into a toolbar.

1. Edit the bitmap that you want to convert to a toolbar by using the bitmap editor.

2. Choose Image⇨Toolbar Editor on the main menu.

3. When the dialog box appears, type the width and height of the toolbar buttons.

4. Click OK. The bitmap image is separated into multiple sections the size of each button, ready for the toolbar editor.

 When you click OK, the bitmap entry moves to the Toolbar section of the resource list. If your bitmap uses more than 16 colors, the color depth decreases to 16.

Unfortunately, you can't size an individual button using this method. Your bitmap should be drawn so it can be split into equal sections.

Common Controls

The Windows operating system provides dynamic link libraries (DLLs) that contain controls any program can use. These *common controls* are actually child windows that an application uses to provide I/O or editing functions. Generally, you use these controls in dialog boxes, but you can use them in other windows.

The controls provide a common user interface between programs. A control from the library looks and acts the same in every program that uses it, shortening the time it takes users to learn a program.

The advantage of a control is that much of the work is done for you, and the more a control does, the less programming you have to do. The edit controls are a good example. These controls provide keyboard processing, cursor movement, and word wrapping, all without your having to write a single line of code.

You can set or retrieve the contents or state of a control by using member functions of the control classes. For a dialog class, the ClassWizard inserts a DoDataExchange() function that exchanges data between controls and member variables. Do not call this function directly; instead, use the UpdateData() member function. The dialog framework calls UpdateData() with a FALSE parameter when a dialog box is created to set the control contents from the member variables, and with a TRUE parameter when you press the OK button to transfer the control contents to the member variables.

Remember: You may call UpdateData() at any point in your code, but it will exchange data among *all* the controls in the DDX function. To retrieve or set the contents or state of a single control, use the control class's member functions.

For a list of the data exchange functions available for each control, refer to the Class Members item in the control's entry in the Help file. Some of the more common functions are listed in the table.

Control	To Set Data	To Retrieve Data	Note
Edit	SetDlgItemText()	GetDlgItemText()	Includes Rich Edit and Static text controls
List box, Combo box	SetItemData()	GetItemData()	32-bit data stored with list item
List and Tree	SetItem()	GetItem()	Requires LV_ITEM structure for List control, TV_ITEM structure for Tree control
	SetItemText()	GetItemText()	Manipulating text
Spinner	SetPos()	GetPos()	For current value
	SetBuddy()	GetBuddy()	Associated up/down buttons
	SetRange()	GetRange()	Limits of control's values
Slider	SetPos()	GetPos()	Current position of slider bar
	SetRangeMin()	GetRangeMin()	Minimum value of slider bar
	SetRangeMax()	GetRangeMax()	Maximum value of slider bar

Creating common controls

The common controls are available via a toolbar that magically appears whenever you create or edit a dialog box. (See the figure below.) Unless you have the dialog box open, you cannot hide or display the Common Controls toolbar.

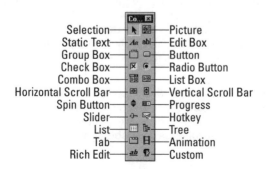

Selection	Picture
Static Text	Edit Box
Group Box	Button
Check Box	Radio Button
Combo Box	List Box
Horizontal Scroll Bar	Vertical Scroll Bar
Spin Button	Progress
Slider	Hotkey
List	Tree
Tab	Animation
Rich Edit	Custom

The table below describes the controls that you can place using the Common Controls toolbar:

To create a common control item in a dialog box, follow these steps:

1. Select the proper control tool from the Common Controls toolbar.

> *Note:* The Common Controls toolbar normally isn't on the toolbar list. The toolbar magically appears whenever you create or edit a dialog box, usually to the right of the screen. While you have the dialog box open, you can hide and display it from the list.

2. Move to the dialog box, and draw the control to the size you want and in the position you want by using the left mouse button. You may adjust the size and location after you draw the control.

3. When you release the mouse button, the control image appears.

Control	MFC Class	Description
Animation	CAnimate	Displays successive frames of an AVI video clip
Button	CButton	Buttons such as OK or Cancel
Combo Box	CComboBox	Edit box and list box combination
Edit Box	CEdit	Boxes for entering text. Often used as the control in a document window
Header	CHeaderCtrl	Button above a column of text Control the width of displayed text
Hotkey	CHotKeyCtrl	Enables user to create a *hot key* to perform an action quickly
Image List	CImageList	Manages large sets of icons or bitmaps (This is not a true control, but it supports lists that other controls use.)
List	CListCtrl	Displays a list of text with icons
List Box	CListBox	Contains a list of strings
Progress	CProgressCtrl	A bar that indicates the progress of an operation
Rich Edit	CRichEditCtrl	Edit control that allows multiple character, paragraph, and color formatting. Often used as the control for a document window
Horizontal/Vertical Scroll Bar	CScrollBar	Scroll bar used inside a dialog box

(continued)

Control	MFC Class	Description
Slider	CSliderCtrl	Similar to a sliding control used as volume control on audio equipment
Spin Button	CSpinButtonCtrl	A pair of arrow buttons to increment or decrement a value
Static Text	CStatic	An edit control for labeling other controls
Status Bar	CStatusBarCtrl	Displays information such as the state of the insert or NumLock keys, or to write status or help messages
Tab	CTabCtrl	Used in property sheets. Similar to notebook tabs.
Toolbar	CToolBarCtrl	Contains buttons to generate command messages
Tool Tip	CToolTipCtrl	A small popup window that describes the use of a button or tool
Tree	CTreeCtrl	Displays a hierarchical list

Adding member variables

When you create a control, you usually need a member control variable to manipulate it. To add a member variable using ClassWizard, follow these steps:

1. Right-click on the control. Select ClassWizard from the popup menu.

2. Select the Member Variables tab of the ClassWizard.

3. Find and select the ID for your control. Click Add Variable.

4. In the popup dialog box, choose Category⇨Control and make sure the Variable Type box shows your control class from the table below.

5. Type the variable name (for example, m_mycombo), and click OK.

6. Add any initialization for the control to the OnInitDialog() function in your dialog class.

The following code shows how you would initialize a list control in OnInitDialog().You would first use the ClassWizard to define a control variable in your class definition:

```
CListCtrl       m_CharList;
```

The example gets its data from an array of structures called ListOfChars, which is read into memory and passed to the CCharList class when it's created. Before executing any code, the function first calls the base class OnInitDialog (). After the

base class call has returned, the dialog box controls have all been
created and are ready for your initialization code.

```
#define      XFLAG        "x"
#define      BLANKFLAG    " "
BOOL CKeyboardDlg::OnInitDialog()
int CCharList::OnInitDialog()
{
int i;
int Widths[] = {115, 77, 70, 35};
const char *Titles [] =
   {
   "Character Name",
   "Position",
   "End Line",
   "Ctrl"
   };
#define           LISTCOLUMNS        (sizeof (Titles)
   / sizeof (char *))

   CDialog::OnInitDialog();
   for (i = 0; i < LISTCOLUMNS; ++i)
      {
   LV_COLUMN      lvc;
      lvc.mask = LVCF_FMT | LVCF_SUBITEM |
   LVCF_TEXT | LVCF_WIDTH;
      lvc.fmt = LVCFMT_LEFT;
      lvc.iSubItem = i;
      lvc.pszText = Titles [i];
      lvc.cx = Widths [i];
      m_CharList.InsertColumn (i, &lvc);
      }
   for (i = 0; i < CHARSET; ++i)
      {
   LV_ITEM    lvi;
   char       text[64];
   int             iActualItem;

      lvi.mask = LVIF_TEXT;
      lvi.iItem = i;
      lvi.iSubItem = 0;
      lvi.lParam = i;
      lvi.pszText = ListOfChars[i].CharName;
      iActualItem = m_CharList.InsertItem(&lvi);

      lvi.iItem = iActualItem;
      lvi.iSubItem = 1;
      sprintf (text, "0x%02X (%d)",
                     ListOfChars[i].Value,
                     ListOfChars[i].Value);
      lvi.pszText = text;
      m_CharList.SetItem(&lvi);
      lvi.iItem = iActualItem;
```

(continued)

(continued)

```
        lvi.iSubItem = 2;
        if (ListOfChars[i].NewLine)
            lvi.pszText = XFLAG;
        else
            lvi.pszText = BLANKFLAG;
        m_CharList.SetItem(&lvi);

        if (ListOfChars[i].Control)
            lvi.pszText = XFLAG;
        else
            lvi.pszText = BLANKFLAG;
        lvi.iItem = iActualItem;
        lvi.iSubItem = 2;
        lvi.pszText = text;
        m_CharList.SetItem(&lvi);
    }
    return TRUE;
                    // return TRUE unless you set the
                    focus
                    // to a control
                    // EXCEPTION: OCX Property Pages
                    should
                    // return FALSE
}
```

How do you know whether to call the base class before or after your code? The ClassWizard inserts some comment text into the body of the function and usually a call to the base class, if required. Watch where it places these comments. If you need to add your code before the base class function call, the wizard will put the comment text before the function call. If the comment text is placed after the base class call, add your code before calling the base class. In the case of `OnInitDialog()`, the base class call must come before your initialization code. (The base function actually creates the controls; if you tried to initialize them before the call, the run code would throw an exception.)

Adding message handlers

Some controls, such as a button, tab, or slider, require message handlers for some of their operations. To add a message handler, use the ClassWizard by following these steps:

1. Right-click on the control, and select ClassWizard from the popup menu.

2. Click the Message Maps tab. In the Object IDs panel, select the resource ID for the control to which you want to add a message handler. The Messages panel lists the messages that are available for the particular control.

3. Select the message you want to add, and click the Add Function button. From the Add Member Function dialog box, give the function a name or click OK to accept the default function name.

4. Click OK, and then select the Edit Code button on the ClassWizard.

5. Add your code to the message handler (similar to the code below).

```
void CMyDialog::OnMyButton()
{
    // TODO: Add your control notification
    handler code here
}
```

If the message has a base class handler, it gets called in this function.

The following example shows how you can set up a message handler to respond to a button labeled "Save Character Set." The resource ID for this button is IDD_LIST_SAVECHARSET. Notice how the ClassWizard has used the components of the ID to build a function name. In this example, the message handler summons another dialog box, the Windows File common dialog box.

```
void CCharList::OnListSavecharset()
{
CString Filter;
int     Index;
FILE    *fp;

    Filter = "Keyboard Files (*.cls)|*.cls||";
    CFileDialog cfd(false, ".cls", NULL,
                    OFN_HIDEREADONLY |
                    OFN_OVERWRITEPROMPT,
                    Filter);
    if (cfd.DoModal () == IDCANCEL)
        return;
    if ((fp = fopen (cfd.GetFileName(), "wb")) ==
    NULL)
    {
        Format = "Cannot open " + cfd.GetFileName( )
                                 + " for writing";
        AfxMessageBox (_T(Text));
        return;
    }
    for (int i = 0; i < CHARSET; ++i)
        fwrite ((char *) &ListOfChars[i], 1,
                sizeof (CHARDEF), fp);
    fclose (fp);
}
```

Dialog Boxes

The dialog box is where users really get into your program. Users don't spend much time with menus and toolbars, but they may spend a lot of time in a dialog box.

Dialog boxes can display records from a file, take input from a user to create some program action, or provide guidance on which direction the program should take. A dialog box can be small with only one or a few controls, or it can fill the entire screen. A dialog box also can be the main window for a program.

Creating a dialog box

To create a dialog box, follow these steps:

1. Select the Resource view panel of the Workspace window and right-click on the top line to summon the menu, or simply type `Ctrl+R`. In the Insert Resource dialog box that pops up, select Dialog from the list.

2. Click the New button. You get a blank dialog box with two buttons: OK and Cancel. You can resize the dialog box to fit your needs. Just grab a corner or edge with the mouse and drag it out to the size you want. Grab the two buttons and drag them to another location if necessary.

3. Right-click on any open area on the new dialog, and select Properties at the bottom of the menu. A four-page form for dialog properties appears.

4. Type an ID. As a convention, dialog box IDs begin with IDD_. Make the name descriptive; you can easily lose track of IDD_DIALOG1, IDD_DIALOG2, and so on. In the Caption field type the title as you want it to appear when the dialog is summoned.

Click the More Styles or Extended Styles tab. I couldn't even hope to cover all the styles and variations here, but you can click the Help icon at the upper-left of the Properties dialog box to get a full explanation of the styles. Try Client edge or Static edge to see what the dialog looks like, or try them both at the same time.

The dialog box is ready for your controls.

Adding a dialog class

Placing dialog boxes into their own separate classes — one class for each dialog box — is convenient and because you'll be adding message handlers and functions to handle your controls. Things get messy if you try to handle more than one in a class. To add the dialog class, follow these steps:

1. Right-click on an open area of the dialog box.

2. From the popup menu, select ClassWizard. In the Adding a Class dialog box, select Create a New Class, and click OK.

3. Give the class a name. Notice the wizard has filled in the base class and resource ID, although you can change them.

4. Click OK. You return to the ClassWizard where you may add variables and functions. Right now there's not a lot to do because you don't have any controls on your dialog (other than the two buttons, and MFC provides message handlers for them).

Your dialog is ready for you to place your own controls on it.

See also "Common Controls" in this part for descriptions of how to use the various controls available to you.

Edit Controls

The basic edit controls are the edit box, rich edit, and static text controls. The first two support the use of only one font in one point size and one color. The rich edit control supports a variety of fonts, sizes, and colors, as well as text formats.

✦ **The edit box control.** This is the basic edit control for Windows programs; you use it wherever a user needs to input text. You can use this control in a view class for editing plain text files or for displaying text where only one font and point size are necessary. The most useful application of the edit box control is in dialog boxes, where data entry usually does not need the capabilities of the rich edit control.

✦ **The rich edit control.** This control includes all the functionality of the edit box control but also supports multiple fonts in various sizes and colors. Originally, the rich edit control was designed to support Word for DOS version 5.0, and it still displays some quirks from that heritage. The introduction of the rich edit control in Windows 95 largely has superseded the edit box control in view classes however, and most applications can benefit from the display capabilities of the rich edit control for view classes.

✦ **The static text control.** This control is not intended for user input. It does not provide for a cursor; generally, you use it to label other controls, primarily in dialog boxes. Unlike the edit box and rich edit controls, this control does not produce a box on the dialog (unless you check one of the frame styles). Instead, the text seems to be written directly on the dialog

background. You draw the control on your dialog box. The
control itself does not contain a label, so you may need to add
a static text control if you need a title for the edit box.

Retrieving text from a text control

Input from an edit control may be retrieved line by line, but most
uses in a dialog box are single-line edit controls. The following
code works for both single- and multiline controls. Add the
following lines to the function where you need to retrieve the text:

```
int LineNumber = LineToRead;
int len = m_MyEdit.LineLength (LineNumber);
char *etext = new char [len + 1];
memset (etext, '\0', len + 1);
m_MyEdit.GetLine (LineNumber, etext, len);
```

In the code above, you need to replace *LineToRead* with an
expression for the line number for the computer to read.
Replace the *m_MyEdit* control with the name that you give to
your control. First, the code uses the LineLength function to
determine the length of the line of code in the m_MyEdit control
and stores the length in the len variable. Then a new array of
characters is declared and the etext variable is set to point at
the first character in the array. Notice the size of the array is set
to one more than the length of the line. The extra array member
holds the NULL character (\0), because the getline() function
doesn't add a NULL terminator. The memset function initializes
the allocated memory to NULL characters, and then the line is
copied into the array.

Remember: Use the delete [] function to free the memory
reserved for etext before exiting the function.

For a single-line control, the line number value is ignored. Set the
buffer to all nulls before getting the text; the control does not
terminate the returned text.

If you need to set or retrieve the contents of an edit control while a
dialog box is displayed, two member functions are useful:

```
GetDlgItemText (UINT ResourceID, char *Buffer, int
    BufferSize);
SetDlgItemText (UINT ResourceID, char *text);
```

If you use CDialog's UpdateData() function, the data in all the
controls of the dialog box is set or retrieved. These functions let
you set or retrieve the contents of a single control.

If you specify the Password style, the characters that a user
enters turn into asterisks (*), but the text that GetLine() or
GetDlgItemText() returns is plain text. You can use the
Password style only in single-line controls.

For a static text control, simply create the control and type in the caption and any styles you want. Generally, that's all there is to a static text control. You can assign the control a variable name and change the text in your program using the SetDlgItemText() member function, but the control is intended to be as its name suggests — static.

Property Sheets

Property sheets are handy when you have a lot of controls for your dialog boxes. On a 640 by 480-pixel display, it's not difficult to design a dialog that fills the entire screen, but it usually doesn't look very good. A more pleasing approach is to break down the controls according to the tasks they perform and then place them on separate pages — *property pages.*

A *property sheet* is the control that holds the property pages. You can create a property page the same way you created a dialog, and then change the base class from CDialog to CPropertyPage when you create the classes. Dialog pages on the sheet would have the base class of CPropertyPage rather than CDialog.

Creating a property sheet

Before you can have property pages, you need a property sheet class to hold your property pages. You don't need a dialog box; Windows takes care of that. The following steps create a property sheet dialog box:

1. Open the ClassWizard (Ctrl+W).

2. Choose Add Class⇨New. Give your property sheet class a name.

3. From the Base Class combo box, select CPropertySheet. Be careful; it's easy to select CPropertyPage by mistake.

4. Click OK, and exit the wizard.

Creating property pages

After you create the property sheet you need to add pages to it. You can't display an empty property sheet. Create the pages as individual dialogs.

1. Open the Insert Resource dialog again (Ctrl+R). Click the + symbol next to Dialog to list the subclasses.

2. Select one of the IDD_PROPPAGE items. It doesn't matter which; you can always resize it. The dialog gives the option because the pages of a property sheet should all be the same size.

TIP

If you do resize a property page, make sure you resize all the pages to match. If you don't, the framework does it, and your controls may end up in strange places.

3. Select New, and your first property page gets created. On this dialog box, the caption is the title that appears on the tab, so keep it short but descriptive.

Prepare as many property pages as you want or need. (Be reasonable, though; think about the poor overloaded memory in your computer.) Each page is a separate dialog. You should have at least two pages. Although you may have seen one-page property sheets, such pages are usually created that way for looks.

Create a class for each page by summoning the ClassWizard (Ctrl+W). Give the class a name, and from the Base Class combo box, select CPropertyPage. Click OK, and exit the ClassWizard.

Adding property pages to a property sheet

You need to add the property pages to your property sheet. Unfortunately, there's no wizard to do this for you. You have to open the header and source files for the property sheet class you created earlier.

1. In the property sheet header file, add a line near the top to include the property page class definition. Assuming the property page header file is called FirstPage.h, type

```
#include "FirstPage.h"
```

2. Scroll down to the protected area of the property sheet class definition, and enter a variable for the property page class. If you called the class CFirstPage, then the line should read

```
CFirstPage m_firstpage;
```

3. You're done with the header file. Go to the property sheet source file, and add the following line of code to the constructors. (A property sheet has two constructors; add the line to both. If you are adding a lot of pages, create a member function to add them and call it from each constructor.)

```
AddPage (&m_firstpage);
```

Remember: AddPage takes a pointer to the variable.

You've created a property sheet. Your program has to provide a means of summoning it, usually through an accelerator, a menu, or a tool button — the same way it calls a dialog, but the object created is of the property sheet class.

```
CMyPropertySheet ps(_TEXT("Property Sheet"));
ps.DoModal ( );   // Show the property sheet
```

TIP

The property sheet needs a title, which is passed when it is declared. The _TEXT (or simply _T) converts the string to a type the control can use.

Selection Controls

Selection controls accept user input for the application. Generally, you use these controls in dialog boxes, but you can also place them on the application's main window frame. In fact, having combo boxes on the main frame for such things as font or color selection is common practice.

Most of the controls share general and extended styles: I list them in the following table rather than repeat them for each of the control types. Styles that are specific to a particular control generally appear on the Styles tab of the control's Properties dialog box.

Control Style	Description
Visible	Determines whether the control is visible when the dialog box is first run
Disabled	Determines whether the control displays as disabled (grayed out) when the dialog box is first run
Group	Specifies the first item in a group of controls through which the user can move by using the arrow keys. The next control with this property set to TRUE ends the group and starts the next.
Tabstop	Allows user to move to this control using the tab key
Help ID	Assigns a help ID to the control based on the resource ID

Extended styles are selected on the Extended Styles page. The properties of extended styles are described in the following table.

Property	Description
Client edge	Creates a sunken edge around the control
Static edge	Creates a border around the control
Model frame	Creates a three-dimensional effect around the control
Transparent	Allows a window under the control to be visible through the control
Accept files	Generates a WM_DROPFILES message if the user drops a file on the control
No parent notify	Disallows WM_PARENTNOTIFY message sending to the control

(continued)

Property	Description
Right aligned	Aligns any text on the right side of the control
Right-to-left	Displays in right-to-left reading order (this is for languages such as Hebrew or Arabic)

The edge or frame selection determines the appearance of the control. They may be used singly or in combination with each other.

Button controls

Buttons are simple controls that send messages to the application when you press the control with the mouse button or select it with the tab key. The OK and Cancel buttons on most dialog boxes are examples of button controls.

Buttons need a message-handler function to process the control messages. Add as many buttons as you need, but add a handler routine for each.

See also "Adding message handlers" in this part.

Combo boxes

A combo box gets its name from the fact that it combines an edit box and a list box in one control. With this control, you can give users a prepared list of items in a compact space; only the selected item is visible until you pull down the list. The most common place for a combo box is in a dialog box, but combo boxes also often appear in toolbars. The Wizard Bar contains three combo boxes.

Drawing a combo box is slightly different from drawing other controls. To draw a combo box control, follow these steps:

1. Select the control from the toolbar. Drag the mouse across the area you want the control to appear. Do not include the drop-down area when you draw the combo box.

2. Release the mouse button. A combo box image appears.

3. Press the down button at the right side of the image. The box in the bottom boundary changes from an outline to a solid. Grab this box with the mouse, and drag it down until it fills the area you want the drop-down box to occupy.

Page 2 of the Properties dialog box contains a list box for entering selection items. Press Ctrl+Enter between items; the editor recognizes an ordinary Enter as the end of the list.

In addition to the standard control extended styles, the combo box has a left scroll-bar property. When selected, the scroll bar in the list box plus the control arrow next to the edit box appear on the left side of the combo box.

When the combo box appears, the edit window is blank. If you want it to display an item, call

```
m_mycombo.SetCurSel (int Index);
```

in the OnInitDialog() function.

Reading a combo box is not so direct. First you have to find the index of the selected item by calling

```
int sel = m_mycombo.GetCurSel();
```

If that's all you need, you're done. Often you may need to read a string from the list. To do this, you need the index of the string. The control has functions for these operations, as shown in the following code:

```
int index, len;
    int len = m_combobox.GetLBTextLen (index);
    char *selstr = new char [len + 1];
    m_combobox.GetLBText (index, selstr);
```

Adding 1 to the size of selstr gives an extra byte for the string terminator.

Note: Be sure to use delete[] selstr to free the string before leaving the routine.

If you are reading the data when the dialog box closes, add a message handler for WM_DESTROY and put the code in it. If you try to read it in the class destructor, you get an exception error. When the destructor executes, the controls are deleted. However, the code in a WM_DESTROY message hander is executed before the destructor.

You may store a DWORD number with each item in a combo box list. This can be any n-"ber you want, a pointer to a structure or class object, a time value for a birthday, a price, and so on. Set the number by calling

```
SetItemData(int nIndex, DWORD dwItemData);
```

and retrieve it by calling

```
DWORD MyVal = SetItemData(int nIndex);
```

List box

List boxes are open windows that contain a list of items a user may select. Along with the edit box, it is one of the components that make up a combo box, and it operates much the same as the list portion of a combo box.

The stand-alone list box control has the added feature of being able to select multiple items in the list. To enable multiple selection, select Multiple or Extended in the Selection box on the style tab.

Other useful list box functions appear in the table.

Function	Type	Purpose
GetCount()	int	Returns the number of items in the list box
GetSel (int index)	int	Returns a positive number if the indexed item is selected; 0 if not, and LB_ERR otherwise
GetTopIndex()	int	Returns the index of the first item in the list
GetTextLen (int index)	int	Returns the text length of the item
GetText (int index, char *buffer)	int	Gets the text of the item and returns it in the buffer parameter
SetItemData (int index, DWORD data)	int	Sets the 32-bit storage to the value passed in the data parameter
GetItemData (int index)	**DWORD**	Retrieves the 32-bit storage from the list box item

The list box control also has a handy function that allows you to list a directory with a single call. The syntax is m_mylistbox.Dir(UINT attr, char *filter). The attribute may be any of the following:

- ✦ CFile::normal
- ✦ CFile::readOnly
- ✦ CFile::hidden
- ✦ CFile::system
- ✦ CFile::volume
- ✦ CFile::directory
- ✦ CFile::archive

The filter is the selection criteria and may contain wildcards. For example, *.exe lists only executables. You can use the OR attribute (|) to get a combination. For example, using the OR attribute with 0x4000 includes a list of drives, along with the files. The filter m_mylistbox.Dir (CFile::normal | 0x4000, "*.cpp"); gives a list of all the .cpp files in the current directory, and a list of all the drives on your system.

Using the OR attribute (|) with 0x8000 restricts the list to the attribute you set. As a default, CFile::normal files are included despite the attribute, but 0x8000 restricts the list to the attribute you pass to the function.

You can use successive calls to this function, but unchecking the Sort style is a good idea. For example,

```
m_mylistbox.Dir(0x4000 | 0x8000, "*");
m_mylistbox.Dir(CFile::directory | 0x8000, "*.*");
m_mylistbox.Dir(CFile::normal, "*.cpp");
```

gives a list beginning with drives on the system, subdirectories in the current directory, and then all .cpp files in the directory, in that order. This method is fairly common in Windows programs.

List controls

Don't confuse the *list* control with the *list box* control. The list box control was a part of the Common Controls long before Windows 9*x*. The list control, however, is a different animal and was introduced with Windows 95. You see this control all through Windows 9*x*. Opening a folder from the desktop, for example, displays a list control. The list control allows you to create a window to list items along with icons to represent the list items.

You can choose from four methods of listing items in a list control:

+ **Icon view:** Displays the items with large icons, each with a label. This is similar to the view of the files you see when you open a folder. Items may be dragged to another location.

+ **Small Icon view:** Lists the items in columns, each with a small icon. This is the same view you get by selecting it under the View menu of a folder. Items may be dragged to another location.

+ **List view:** Lists the items in a single column. List item may not be dragged.

+ **Report view:** Each item appears in a column with an icon and label. Additional columns allow you to list information about the item. This is the view you get when you choose View➪ Details in a folder. You cannot drag items to another location.

Progress bars

This control doesn't do any real work, but it does give user feedback when performing long operations. The code to support a progress bar isn't complex, but the return is high for a user's peace of mind.

Setting up and using a progress bar takes only a few lines of code. As long as the bar advances, you know the code is working. You can put a progress bar in a toolbar.

In the `OnInitDialog()` function, add the following lines:

```
m_myprogbar.SetRange (MIN_VALUE, MAX_VALUE);
m_myprogbar.SetPos (INITIAL_VALUE);
m_myprogbar.SetStep (STEP_VALUE);
```

At key places in your code, make a call to `m_myprogbar.StepIt` `()` and the progress bar will increment by `STEP_VALUE`.

See also the sample code under "Sliders" for an example of using a progress bar.

Radio buttons

This control has been around for a long time. In MFC, it derives its properties from `CButton`. The radio buttons control takes its name from the fact that it acts like the selection buttons on a car radio — you can select only one button at a time.

Some important rules to remember when creating radio buttons:

✦ Create all the radio buttons in a group in sequence. Do not create any other controls between buttons. This assures their grouping in the resource file declaration of the dialog box.

✦ On the first button, check the `Group` property on the General styles page. This marks the button as the first in the group. On subsequent buttons in this group, do not check the box.

✦ If this is not the last control to be created, check the `Group` property on the next nonradio button control. This marks the end of the radio button sequence.

Scroll bars

Use a scroll bar when the text or object in a window is too large to display completely. MFC classes normally add scroll bars automatically when you select the `AUTOHSCROLL` or `AUTOVSCROLL` style flags.

You may use a scrollbar as an indicator, similar to a progress bar, or for user input, similar to a slider.

Sliders

These controls look like the sliding volume controls on audio/visual equipment. In fact, you can make them serve the same purpose (as in the Windows 9x Volume Control utility program).

Sliders need some initialization, so I'll guide you through the steps of creating some sample code. I show you how your program can read and set sliders and combine it with a progress bar just to show some results. To add a slider to your application, follow these steps and insert your own values. Instead of a progress bar, you can use the slider values to operate on any control.

1. On your dialog box, create vertical and horizontal sliders. The default for a slider is horizontal. Now draw a progress bar using the progress bar control tool. You'll make the two sliders track each other and show their positions using the progress bar.

2. Summon the ClassWizard (Ctrl+W is a quick way), and add variables for these three objects, for example, m_vertslider, m_horzslider, and m_progbar. Make sure your dialog box has message handlers for WM_INITDIALOG, WM_HSCROLL, and WM_VSCROLL.

3. Add the following #define near the top of your source file:

```
#define MAX_SLIDER_VALUE    100
```

4. In the OnInitDialog() function, add the following code:

```
m_horzslider.SetRange (0, MAX_SLIDER_VALUE);
m_horzslider.SetPos (0);
m_horzslider.SetTicFreq (10);
m_vertslider.SetRange (0, MAX_SLIDER_VALUE);
m_vertslider.SetPos (MAX_SLIDER_VALUE);
m_vertslider.SetTicFreq (10);
m_progbar.SetRange (0, MAX_SLIDER_VALUE);
m_progbar.SetPos (0);
```

The initial position of the vertical slider in this example is MAX_SLIDER_VALUE instead of 0. Curiously, Microsoft created the control with 0 at the top and full value at the bottom, just the opposite of the way sliders are used in the real world.

The tick frequency is set to 10. With Autotick on and a range of 100, the ticks are so close together they make a black bar. Add space between the ticks by calling SetTicFreq().

5. Now link the two sliders. In the OnHScroll() message handler, add the following:

```
if ((CSliderCtrl *) pScrollBar ==
  &m_horzslider)
{
   int pos = m_horzslider.GetPos();
   m_vertslider.SetPos (MAX_SLIDER_VALUE -
   pos);
```

(continued)

Selection Controls

(continued)

```
        m_progbar.SetPos (pos);
        return;
}
CDialog::OnHScroll(nSBCode, nPos, pScrollBar);
```

The first line tests whether this is the horizontal slider. All scroll-bar, slider, and spin-button messages pass through this handler. The third parameter is a pointer to the actual control. The type, however, is CScrollBar*, so you have to cast it to CSliderCtrl*. If it isn't your slider, then just call the default handler and return. *See also* Part VI.

The next line reads the position of the horizontal slider. Next, you set the vertical slider position to match the horizontal slider and indicate the positions in the progress bar.

Remember: If you are using a vertical slider, override the OnVScroll() handler. The code is slightly different. (Don't forget that you need to adjust for the top-to-bottom behavior.)

```
if ((CSliderCtrl *) pScrollBar == &m_vertslider)
{
    pos = MAX_SLIDER_VALUE - m_vertslider.GetPos();
    m_horzslider.SetPos (pos);
    m_scrollbar.SetScrollPos (pos);
    m_progbar.SetPos (pos);
    return;
}
CDialog::OnVScroll(nSBCode, nPos, pScrollBar);
```

Compile and run your program. Summon the dialog box. As you move one slider, the other tracks with it, and the progress bar indicates the relative position of the sliders.

To hide the tick marks on the right side or the bottom, make the control slimmer. If you don't have enough room for tick marks on both sides, the control draws only the top or left tick marks.

Spin buttons

You often use the spin button control (or *spinner*) with an edit box to display a number. The spinner gets its name from the way the values spin up or down as you hold down one of the buttons.

You may attach a spinner to another window to display values, or you can use it to control the display in any control. The buttons generate either a WM_HSCROLL or WM_VSCROLL message, depending on the orientation of the buttons. You have to sort it out from any other scroll controls. The third parameter to the scroll message handler is a pointer to the control that caused it. Use the following test to determine if the message was generated by your control:

```
if ((CSpinButtonCtrl *) pScrollBar == &m_myspinner)
{
// Add your code to handle the spinner
    return;
}
```

Remember: Don't forget the return statement in this part of the code; you don't want the dialog box to process it as a normal scroll message.

If you are going to attach a spinner to another control using the Auto Buddy property, create the other control first and then the spinner control. Do *not* create any other controls in between, or the spinner will attach to the wrong control.

For an example, use the code in the section on sliders, but substitute a spinner for one of the sliders.

Tab controls

The tab control is like the tabs in a notebook. The Help system isn't very informative about these controls. You can study the example programs in Visual C++, but they have almost no comments in them to explain how to use the various functions.

To use the tab control, follow these steps:

1. Create a tab control by drawing it on your dialog box.

2. Put a control variable in the class for your dialog box.

3. Put the following code in the OnInitDialog() function.

```
TC_ITEM TabItem;
TabItem.mask = TCIF_TEXT;
TabItem.pszText = "First";
m_tab.InsertItem (0, &TabItem);
```

4. Repeat the last two lines of code for as many tabs as you need, changing to the title that will appear on the tab.

When a user selects a tab, Windows sends a TCN_SELCHANGE message to your application. Add a message handler to and call the tab control to get the newly selected tab.

```
int sel = m_tab.GetCurSel();
```

You can put different controls on each of the tab pages, but you have to show and hide each control as the page gets and loses focus. For this reason, tab pages are best suited for only one — or a few at best — controls. If you have several controls you want to place on a tab page, you can create another dialog box and place it on the tab page.

The tab control is the basis of the property sheets you see all throughout Windows 9x. The property sheet, however, is a stand-alone dialog box, but you may place a tab control in any dialog box along with other controls.

Tree controls

You need look only as far as the Workspace window to see a tree control example. Building a tree control is not difficult, but it is a tedious task. The tedium can get to you, and bugs can creep in, so test your tree often to make sure it's growing in the right direction.

The best way to describe a tree is by building a sample. When you have a working tree, you can copy and paste the code into other programs and then change the values and text for your own needs. To create a sample tree, follow these steps:

1. Draw the tree control on your dialog box. Make the control about 1$^{1}/_{2}$ inches wide by 2 inches deep.

2. Select the following styles: Has Buttons, Has Lines, Lines At Root and Border. (After you see the basic tree, try changing these styles to see the effects.)

3. Type the ClassWizard, and create a member variable in your class for the tree object.

4. You need a structure to insert tree items, so in the `OnInitDialog()` function, add the following variable:

```
TV_INSERTSTRUCT        TreeItem;
```

5. Add a root node, also in `OnInitDialog()`, and call it "Animals".

```
TreeItem.hParent = TVI_ROOT;
TreeItem.hInsertAfter = TVI_LAST;
TreeItem.item.mask = TVIF_TEXT | TVIF_PARAM;
TreeItem.item.pszText = "Animals";
TreeItem.item.lParam = 0;
HTREEITEM hAnimal1 =
   m_tree.InsertItem(&TreeItem);
```

6. Now add a root node for "Plants".

```
TreeItem.item.pszText = "Plants";
TreeItem.item.lParam = 1;
HTREEITEM hPlant1 =
   m_tree.InsertItem(&TreeItem);
```

`TVI_ROOT` specifies this is a root node. The `hInsertAfter` member is the handle of the node to insert this item under. You could insert the handle of another object here, but you may use the following predefined handles:

♦ TVI_FIRST: Inserts the item at the beginning of the list under the parent node.

♦ TVI_LAST: Inserts the item at the end of the list under the parent node.

♦ TVI_SORT: Inserts the item into the list under the parent node in alphabetical order.

The "item" member is a TV_ITEM structure within TV_INSERTSTRUCT. This is the information the control stores with the item.

TVIF_TEXT | TVIF_PARAM means you are going to insert text and a parameter. The text, the pszText line, is what appears in the tree. The lParam is a 32-bit number of your choice; use it to identify and act on the tree item.

The HTREEITEM casts a variable to a handle that you will use as the parent for subsequent entries under this node.

Compile and test your dialog box. Make sure you have two root nodes on the list ("Animals" and "Plants"). Compile and test often, especially after any major node change. After you test the root nodes, continue building the tree by adding subnodes.

1. Add a subnode for "Domesticated" animals.

```
TreeItem.hParent = hAnimal1;
TreeItem.item.pszText = "Domesticated";
TreeItem.item.lParam = 100;
HTREEITEM hDomestic =
   m_tree.InsertItem(&TreeItem);
```

2. Add a subnode for "Wild and Free" animals.

```
TreeItem.item.pszText = "Wild and Free";
TreeItem.item.lParam = 110;
HTREEITEM hWildFree =
   m_tree.InsertItem(&TreeItem);
```

3. Now add some animals under "Domesticated".

```
TreeItem.hParent = hDomestic;
TreeItem.item.pszText = "Dogs";
TreeItem.item.lParam = 111;
m_tree.InsertItem(&TreeItem);


TreeItem.item.pszText = "Cats";
TreeItem.item.lParam = 112;
m_tree.InsertItem(&TreeItem);
```

(continued)

(continued)

```
TreeItem.item.pszText = "Hamsters";
TreeItem.item.lParam = 113;
m_tree.InsertItem(&TreeItem);
```

4. Add some animals under "Wild and Free".

```
TreeItem.hParent = hWildFree;
TreeItem.item.pszText = "Tigers";
TreeItem.item.lParam = 111;
m_tree.InsertItem(&TreeItem);


TreeItem.item.pszText = "Platypus";
TreeItem.item.lParam = 112;
m_tree.InsertItem(&TreeItem);
```

Notice that each item has its own value for
TreeItem.item.lParam. Anytime that node is selected, you can
retrieve the value by calling

```
HTREEITEM hTree = m_tree.GetSelectedItem ();
DWORD data = m_tree.GetItemData (hTree);
```

Using that value, you can write a switch statement to show a
picture, play a sound, or perform some other action based on the
tree entry.

I'll leave it to you to create the hierarchy for plants. I'm tired of
climbing trees.

Wizards

Wizards are neat tools for programmers. The important concept of
a wizard is that the user must go through the pages in order rather
than select a page or control at random. If one step relies on
information to be supplied on an earlier page, you can disable the
Next button until that information is provided. You deal with
plenty of wizards in Visual C++. Actually, a wizard is nothing more
than a property sheet with a "Wizard Mode" flag turned on.

Maybe it's time you became a wizard, or learned to create one.
First, you need to create a property sheet with at least two tabs.

See also "Property Sheets" in this part.

Creating a wizard

To build a wizard from a property sheet, follow these steps:

1. Open the source file for your property sheet class (*not* a page class). Zip up to the Wizard Bar, and click on the down arrow on the Action button. From the drop-down menu, select Add Virtual Function.

2. In the dialog, find and select DoModal in the New Virtual Functions panel.

3. Click the Add and Edit button. Add the following line of code to the newly created DoModal() function *before* the call to the base class DoModal():

```
SetWizardMode();
```

That's all there is to it. Recompile your program, and run it. Summon what once was a property sheet. (Pretend to toss smoke dust into the fire at the same time.) You should notice the following changes:

What used to be the titles on the tabs are now the dialog titles as you step through the pages. Instead of OK, Cancel, and Apply buttons, you now have Back, Next, and Cancel.

Your last page should provide some means of completing the wizard steps without having to press Cancel.

Making the Finish button appear

Now for some befuddling Microsoft magic. (Okay, you run into this in the Borland IDE, as well.) On the last page you want the second button to read Finish instead of Next. You need to call SetWizardButtons() with some flags to change it. The Help file reads, "Typically, you should call SetWizardButtons from CPropertyPage::OnSetActive." Nice, considering SetWizardButtons is a member of CPropertySheet, *not* CPropertyPage, and you can't call it from your page class. The base class also has no variable to identify the property sheet that created it.

You can use several methods to get to SetWizardButtons(), but the best one seems to use one of the class casting macros, either STATIC_DOWNCAST or DYNAMIC_DOWNCAST. These macros cast one object to another. Use the macro to get the CWnd parent, and then cast it to CPropertySheet, which is the base class for your parent.

Add the OnSetActive virtual function using the Wizard Bar Action button to the *last* property page. Put the following lines of code into it:

```
CpropertySheet* ps =
    STATIC_DOWNCAST(CPropertySheet, GetParent());
ps->SetWizardButtons(PSWIZB_BACK | PSWIZB_FINISH);
```

Do the same thing for the next-to-last property page, except make the function call

```
ps->SetWizardButtons(PSWIZB_BACK | PSWIZB_NEXT);
```

This makes the Finish button appear on the last page but resets it to Back if the user goes to the previous page.

In a wizard, you may run into a number of circumstances where you need to access functions in the parent class. I prefer to add the property sheet pointer as a member of the property page class and then use the macro in OnInitDialog(). This tactic makes the pointer available in all member functions.

If you don't include a flag, the button becomes disabled. Add the OnSetActive function to your *first* property page, and add the same code. Disable the Back button with the following line of code:

```
ps->SetWizardButtons(PSWIZB_NEXT);
```

The flag parameter to SetWizardButtons() may be any combination of the following:

Flag Parameter	*Button*
PSWIZB_BACK	The Back button
PSWIZB_NEXT	The Next Button
PSWIZB_FINISH	The Finish Button
PSWIZB_DISABLEDFINISH	The Finish button (disabled)

Next and Finish share the same button. You may have one or the other for a wizard page but not both.

Part V

The Help Workshop

From an end user's point of view, preparing a good Help file is one of the most important tasks you need to perform in your programming project. From a programmer's view, the Help file is your platform for explaining how to use your program, and a good Help file can save you many hours of time spent helping users. Unfortunately, the Help file is missing from most Windows programming books. Even in books that do talk about Help files, the topic usually gets just a glancing blow.

In this part . . .

- ✔ Compiling Help files
- ✔ Editing Help files
- ✔ Exploring the Help Workshop's Help file
- ✔ Using rich text editors
- ✔ Using Visual C++ Help tools
- ✔ The Windows Help Engine
- ✔ Writing effective Help

Compiling Help Files

As with any programming effort, compile and test Help projects often. The Help Workshop isn't as easy to use as Visual C++ when locating errors, so try to catch and correct any potential problems quickly.

The Help compiler isn't as fast as the Visual C++ compiler, either. On large projects, having to wait 10 to 15 minutes for a compile isn't uncommon. The Help compiler has a lot of work to do in building its internal file system, compiling your topic files, and including bitmaps and other files. Outfitting your development computer with additional RAM reduces wait time.

To compile a Help project, follow these steps:

1. In the Help Workshop, choose File➪Compile or press the Compile button on the toolbar. The project file doesn't have to be open to compile it.

2. In the dialog box that pops up, the Project File combo box contains a list of recently opened Help projects. Select the one you want to compile. The list below summarizes the options on this dialog box:

- The Minimize Window When Compiling option hides the window during the compilation. Microsoft's literature says this option speeds up the compilation, but that's academic on machines with adequate memory. Anyway, watching a compilation is pretty boring, so minimizing the window is a good idea.

- The Automatically Display Help File in WinHelp When Done is ho-hum. This option causes the compiler to automatically start WinHelp and display your Help file after the compile. More often than not, you may want to look at the results of the compilation, and starting a test view of the Help file isn't difficult.

- Select Turn off Compression when you're compiling your Help files for testing. This action greatly speeds compile time, sometimes by 25 to 50 percent. Of course, on the final compilation you should leave compression turned on.

- The Include .rtf Filename and Topic ID in Help File option is a handy debugging aid. Selecting this check box causes two new fields to appear in the Topic Information dialog box (the dialog box you get when you right-click a topic ID and select Topic Information from the menu). These new fields contain the .rtf file the topic is in and the topic's ID and can speed debugging. Make sure you deselect this box when you compile your Help file for release.

To use the Include .rtf Filename and Topic ID in Help File option, you must have Help Author mode turned on.

See also the "Testing Help Files" section in this chapter for a description of Help Author mode.

Creating a Help Project

To prepare a Help file, you need one or more topic files — the files produced by a rich text editor such as Word or WordPerfect. These topic files contain the actual messages that will appear in your help windows. You can't compile a Help project without a topic file, but you can create a project without it.

Also, you don't need an application to have a Help project, although generally a user will launch a Help file by using links in an application.

The MFC AppWizard gives you a head start in creating a Help file, but you don't have to use it. The following list explains your options.

+ Selecting "Context sensitive help" in Step 4 of the MFC AppWizard when you create a new project makes the wizard prepare several basic files for your Help project: the Help project file, a contents file, a map file, a topics file, and several bitmaps to illustrate the Help windows. Look for these files in the "HLP" subdirectory where you created your application.

+ If you didn't select Context Help in the AppWizard, you still can create a Help project. At times, you may want to prepare a Help file but really don't need an application. For example, as I get older and more senile, I need help jogging my memory; so I have created some personal Help files. One of these files contains code snippets for using the various common controls that Windows provides. No application is associated with it, so to run it, I simply click the desktop icon I created for it or run "winhelp controls.hlp" from the command line.

Except for the rich text files (the topic files), don't directly edit the Help files that the MFC AppWizard creates. Several of the Help files are sensitive to stray spaces and tabs. Use a rich text editor such as Word or WordPerfect to edit the topic files, and use the Help Workshop to modify the other files.

See also "Help Workshop Help File" and "Editing Help Files" in this part.

As your application develops, the Workshop makes changes to some of these files, adding Help IDs for dialog boxes and controls, and so forth. You, of course, have to write the actual text for the Help topics.

To create a Help project, follow these steps:

1. Choose Start⇨Help Workshop.

2. Choose File⇨New⇨Help Project, and then click OK.

3. Specify the path and file name for your project, and then click Save.

4. Add the Help project information to the files using the buttons on the right side of the project window. If you created your topic files (the rich text files), click the Files button. If the files are in the same directory in which you created the Help project, select the files and click the Add button, and select the path and file to add to your project. Otherwise, you need to browse to the files. Continue until you include all the files.

   Note: If you haven't created your topic files yet, you need to return to this step after you create the topic files to add them to the project.

5. Continue adding elements to your project as needed by using the Help Project Window buttons that appear in the table.

When you open the project in the Help Workshop, you see a window with an array of buttons down the right side, regardless of whether you created your own basic Help files or had the MFC AppWizard prepare them for you. Here's what the buttons mean:

Help Project Window Button	Purpose
Options	Specify options for compressing files, sorting keywords, text search functionality, macros, fonts, and build tags.
Files	Specify the location of the topic (rich text) files. You cannot compile a Help project without specifying at least one topic file.
Windows	Set the type, attribute, color, and position of Help windows; and specify which buttons should appear on the Help windows and which macros should run when the window displays. You can use macros, for example, to change the color of the window.
Bitmaps	If your Help file includes bitmaps as illustrations (always a good idea, especially for complicated dialog boxes and toolbars), use this button to specify their location. Use the Segmented Hypergraphics Editor (shg.exe) to put hotspots on your graphics for mouse clicks. (See the section on Hypergraphics in this chapter.)
Map	Use to associate topic IDs with numeric values. The association is required for context-sensitive help.

Help Project Window Button	Purpose
Alias	Replace one set of topic IDs with another.
Config	Specify menus or buttons to appear on the Help windows or to register DLL (Dynamic Link Library) functions.
Data Files	Files to include in the Help file system. Placing files in the internal file system (as opposed to the Windows file system) makes access faster, but increases the size of the Help file.
Save and Compile	Saves the modifications to the Help project and compiles the project into a Help (.hlp) file.

Microsoft didn't include a separate Save button. Often, you may find yourself making changes without being ready to recompile the project. Simply closing the project file gives the option to save without compiling. You can then reopen the project.

The contents file

A contents file isn't a requirement for a Help project, but it does add some pep and energy to your project. For large applications, you may need a contents file as the place to link several Help files together.

The Windows Help Engine uses the contents file to generate that nifty tree control with open and closed book icons on the Help Topics dialog box. The contents file also can contain links to multiple Help files. If your project contains several components, you can provide links to the Help files in the contents file, even for Help files that do not exist yet. When you run the Help Engine, it looks for the files linked in the contents; if it doesn't find them, the items containing the links do not display.

The contents file is a plain text file, and you can edit it using a program such as Notepad. However, the indenting and links can get confusing for large projects, so the best approach is to maintain it, using the Help Workshop editor.

To create a contents file:

1. In the Help Workshop, choose File⇨New.

2. In the New dialog box, you have the choice of selecting a project file or a contents file from the list box. Select "Help Contents" from the list box, and press the OK button.

The dialog box that appears is the same dialog box you use when you later edit your contents file, so the following steps apply to editing as well as to creating a file.

3. Type the name of the file that contains most of your Help topics in the Default Filename field.

4. In the Default Title field, enter the text you want to appear in the title bar of the Help Topics dialog box. This title appears in Help windows that do not have a title specified in the [WINDOWS] section of the project file. You also can enter the title by clicking the Edit button and filling in the fields.

5. Click the Add Above or Add Below button to enter your first heading or topic. Because you haven't added topics to the list yet, you can select either button. However, after adding your first topic, you need to select one or the other, depending on where you want the new topic to appear.

6. Select the Heading or Topic radio button from the Edit Contents Tab Entry. When the contents file is invoked from your application, a book icon will represent Heading. When you double-click the icon, the icon changes to an open book to reveal the items below it. A page icon will represent a topic; double-click the icon and the topic window. Other radio button options are "Macro" to run a predefined macro when you click the item and "Include" to link another contents file to this one.

If you make a mistake here or later want to change the level type, you can't change it. You have to delete it by using the Remove button and reinserting the item with the correct type.

7. In the Title edit box, enter the title as you want it to appear in the topic tree control. If this is a heading entry, all the other fields become disabled. If it is a topic, enter the ID of the topic in the Topic ID field. This is the ID you use with the "#" keyword in your topic files, and the ID should not contain any spaces. Generally, try to use the resource ID or Help ID provided by the Workshop; things can get confusing in a large project. Also in this dialog box, enter the Help filename (if it is not the default file) in which the topic is located in the Help File edit box and the window type you want to use in the Window Type edit box. (It's okay to leave the Window Type blank if you haven't created a window type; the workshop will use a default.)

8. Click Move Right or Move Left to adjust the indent level of the item. The indent level is important. If an item is indented to the right more than the item above it, it appears as a subitem. The display shows you the relative position of items.

9. Repeat the above steps until you have entered all the headings and topics you want to appear on your Help Topics page.

You should be aware of three other buttons at the bottom of the dialog box, but you probably won't need them for beginning Help projects:

✦ **Tabs:** Use to display custom tabs in the dialog box. To use this, you have to write your own DLL specifically for this purpose.

✦ **Link Files:** Use to list other files if your Help file contains A-Link and K-Link macros that jump to topics in those files

✦ **Index Files:** Use to list other Help files whose keywords should appear in the Index tab of the Help Topics dialog box. The Help compiler searches for keywords in your Help files to build the index.

Making new window types

To a limited extent, you can customize your topic windows in the Help system. You can change the color and appearance of the scrolling and nonscrolling portions of the windows to give your Help file a distinctive appearance.

To define a new window type:

1. Click the Windows button on the Help Project dialog box. The Window Properties property sheet appears.

2. Click the Add button on the General tab to create a new window type.

3. In the Add A New Window dialog box that appears, enter a name for your window type. The name must be eight characters or fewer. Leave the standard window types box on "Procedure."

4. Click the Position tab to set up the window size and position.

5. For now, press the Auto Sizer button. Drag the sample window to the position on the screen where you want it to appear, and then grab the edges of the window to size it to your needs. Click the OK button on the sample window. Later, you can adjust the size by entering new values in the Left, Top, Width, and Height edit boxes.

6. Select the Buttons tab, and check the buttons you want to appear on your window.

7. Click the Color tab. Notice the two areas of your window — the nonscrolling region and the scrolling region. The scrolling region is the region that contains the actual text for the topic when the Help window is displayed. Click the Change button next to either region to change its color. The "Choose Color"

common dialog box appears. After you select a color, click OK on the color dialog box. The background of the region should change to your selected color.

8. If you want to add macros that execute when the window type you are creating displays, add them on the Macro tab.

9. Return to the General tab and give your window a title. The "Comment" field is not used in the Help file and is intended as a note to yourself. Checking the "Auto-size height" box causes the window to expand or shrink automatically to fit the text. Checking "Keep Help window on top" makes the window stay in the foreground, even if the user returns to the application without closing the Help file.

Editing Help Files

By using a rich text editor such as WordPerfect or Microsoft Word, you can create all the subtle codes that make the Help file work. The compiler needs special symbols and text attributes to create such things as jump targets and browse sequences.

Footnotes

You create much of a Help file's action by using footnotes. A unique mark identifies each footnote; the mark has significance to the Help compiler. The accompanying table explains the marks.

Mark	Character	Purpose	Footnote Example
Poundal	#	Defines a unique topic identifier. It is required for all topics. Should be the Help ID for the topic.	# IDH_MYDIALOG
Dollar	$	Denotes the title of a topic as it will appear in the "Topics Found" dialog box, the Bookmark dialog box, and the history window.	$ My Dialog Box

Mark	Character	Purpose	Footnote Example
Plus	+	With a number value, defines the topic's position in a browse sequence. Index:0005 identifies this as the fifth in the Index browse sequence. You can leave gaps between numbers for later expansion.	+ Index:0005
Exclamation	!	Defines a macro that is to run when the user opens the topic. SetPopupColor (255,255,200), for example, causes a pop-up window to appear with a light yellow background.	! SetPopupColor (255,255,200)
Asterisk	*	Defines topics used in conditional builds.	* DEBUGBUILD
Greater than	>	Identifies a window type for the topic. This is a window type defined in the Help Workshop. See the section on Creating New Window Types under Creating Help Projects.	> MyWindow
A	A	Specifies words used in ALink macros. An ALink is similar to a KLink, but the identifier does not appear in the index of the Help Topics dialog box. The Help system uses an ALink internally.	A Link Name
K	K	Specifies words used in KLink macros. A KLink appears in the index of the Help Topics dialog box, and a user can access it by clicking on the entry.	K Link Name

To insert a footnote using Microsoft Word:

1. Choose Insert⇨Footnote.

2. In the dialog box that pops up, make sure you select the Footnote radio button. In the Numbering section, select Custom Marks and enter a footnote character from the table above.

3. Click OK, and type the text of your footnote next to the mark. If you have View⇨Footnotes on, the footnote appears in a window at the bottom of the screen.

In WordPerfect, adding footnotes for a Help file is more difficult. Follow a slightly different sequence:

1. Before you begin, choose Insert⇨Footnote⇨Options. Make sure you select the "Characters" option, and then enter the characters from the chart above. In WordPerfect Version 6.1, this field accepts only five characters, so you may have to alter it occasionally. Also note the sequence of characters. WordPerfect assigns the first character to the first footnote and continues through the list.

2. Create the footnote by choosing Insert⇨Footnote⇨Create.

3. Type the footnote text at the bottom of the page.

Browse sequences

A Browse sequence is the collection and order of topic windows that appears when the user clicks either the "<<" or ">>" buttons at the top of the Help window. You can group windows of similar topics together under a single browse identifier and then set the order in which you want them to appear.

Place a topic in a browse sequence by using a plus sign (+) footnote, giving it the browse sequence identifier, and adding a number in the footnote text. The numbers don't have to be sequential; you may leave gaps for later adjustments and additions, jumping, for example, from number 010 to 020. Browse sequence numbers should have the leading zeros so the numbers are all the same length. Browse sequence identifiers have a limit of 50 characters.

You don't need to include a browse sequence number. If you don't, the compiler creates the browse sequence in the order in which the compiler encounters the topics. If you later need to reorder the sequence, you can add the numbers, but you need to add them to all the topics in the sequence. Make it easy for yourself and always include the numbers.

For example, adding the + footnote to a topic named Spell Menu and placing + `commands:040` in the footnote text assigns the Spell Menu topic to the command browse sequence and gives it the relative number of 40.

Graphics

Adding bitmaps and hypergraphics to your Help file significantly increases the compile time. But a picture is worth a thousand words, and a well-prepared hypergraphic that pops up brief explanations of an object such as a dialog box can make your Help file easier to use.

See also "Segmented Hypergraphics Editor" in this part.

Declare a graphic in your topic file by enclosing its filename inside braces { and } along with the keyword `bml`, `bmr`, or `bmc`. Use those keywords even if you are inserting a hypergraphic (.shg) file.

Syntax	What It Does
{bmc filename.shg}	Places the graphic using character alignment. It is treated just like any other character. If you want to center a graphic by itself in the window, follow the declaration with an end of paragraph, and then use the Center Align command of the rich text editor.
{bml filename.shg}	Positions the graphic along the left margin of the window; flows text around the graphic on the right.
{bmr filename.shg}	Places the graphic on the right margin; flows text around it on the left.

Hotspots

A hotspot is like a Web link. When the user clicks on the hotspot, the Help system jumps to the topic identified in hidden text.

To declare a hotspot:

+ If you want Help to display a new topic when the user clicks on the hotspot, type the text in double-underline mode. In Word, choose Format⇨Font and select Double in the Underline combo box. In WordPerfect, choose Format⇨Font and select the Double Underline check box.

+ If you want Help to display a pop-up window without closing the current topic page, type the link text in single-underlined text. In both Word and WordPerfect, the underline mode is available on a toolbar button.

✦ In either case, *immediately* after the link text, type the topic ID of the new window in hidden text (no intervening spaces). In Word, choose Format⇨Font and select the Hidden check box. In WordPerfect, you have to type the ID in normal text, define it, and then choose Format⇨Font and select the Hidden check box; the Hidden box is disabled unless the text is defined.

In the compiled Help file, the link text appears in green. When the user clicks on the link, the Help system jumps to the topic identified in the hidden text or displays a pop-up box, depending upon the underline mode.

Creating links

Help provides two macros, KLink and ALink, to provide jumps to multiple topics based on keywords rather than specific context strings. Because you resolve the jumps at runtime rather than when you compile the file, you can create jumps between Help files. You also can provide jumps to Help files that may have changed since the original compilation of the Help project.

The KLink macro uses K-keywords, which are in the index. The ALink macro is identical except it uses A-keywords, which never appear in the index. These macros can access multiple Help files when specified in the contents file.

See also "Footnotes" in this section for steps to add A- and K-type keywords.

The syntax for both macros is the same:

```
KLink(keyword[;keyword],type,topic ID,Window Type)
```

The macro requires at least one keyword; the rest of the parameters are optional. A keyword may contain a comma if the keyword is enclosed in quotes. Use a semicolon to separate multiple keywords.

In the macro, topic ID can take one of four values, as shown in the table. Notice that the number 3 doesn't exist. The Help Workshop Help could lead you to believe that you can use the name (for example, TITLE) as the topic ID parameter, but with my version of the workshop, only the number value seems to work.

Number Value	Name	Description
0	Place holder	You can't have empty parameters. If you omit a parameter and have a parameter following it, you must have a number in this position. 0 fills the bill.

Number Value	Name	Description
1	JUMP	If only one keyword is found, Help jumps directly to that topic.
2	TITLE	If Help finds a keyword in more than one Help file, the title of the file appears next to the topic in the Topics Found dialog box.
4	TEST	Returns 0 if no match was found or 1 if one or more matches were found.

Topic ID specifies the ID to display in a pop-up window if Help does not find a match. Without this parameter, the message box "No additional help is available" displays if no match is found.

Window **Type** specifies the name of a window to use when the topic displays. If blank, the default type is used; otherwise, *Window Type* should be the name of a window you defined. (See "Making new window types" in the section on "Creating a Help Project.")

Replace missing parameters with empty quotation marks (except *Type*, which must be a number), but don't end the parameter string with a comma. If parameters are left off at the end, simply end the string without any trailing commas.

Add the macro to your contents file by using the following steps:

1. Open the contents file in the Help Workshop.

2. Determine where you want to place the macro, and select the item either just before or just after that point.

3. Press the Add Above or Add After button, as appropriate.

4. Select the Macro radio button. In the Title field, enter the text as you want it to appear in the contents list.

5. Enter the macro in the Macro field, including all parameters as you want them to be used. Click OK.

When you examine the contents file, you find the Workshop has truncated the name of the macro to AL or KL. This is fine; the Help system recognizes on the first two characters of a macro name.

Macros

The Help system contains a number of predefined macros you can use in your Help file. Add these macros to your project by using the exclamation point (!) footnote. Use only one "!" footnote. If you want to run more than one macro, include them in the same footnote, separated by a semicolon in the order in which you want them to run.

I can't list all of the many macros here, but if you choose
Help⇨Help Topic and type **macros**, you get a list of them. Select
the one that interests you, and double-click it. Take a look at some
of the most useful macros:

✦ JumpContents: Jump to the contents topic of another Help
  file. Using this macro is an easy way to link Help files, but you
  should make certain the other file is present, or Help will
  display an error.

✦ SetPopupColor: Sets the background color of pop-up
  windows. The default is white, but this parameter lets you
  specify any combination of the three colors. SetPopupColor
  (255,255,255) gives the pop-up window a slightly yellowish
  cast, for example.

✦ ShellExecute: Allows you to open a file outside the Help
  system and pass it parameters. If the file is an executable file,
  it runs. If it is a document file, it opens or prints, according to
  the macro flags.

✦ ShortCut: Runs a specified program or, if it already is
  running, activates it. Parameters allow you to send the
  program a command through the WM_COMMAND message.

✦ IfThen: Allows you to test a macro's return value and run it
  or another if the value is non-zero. IfThen(MacroToTest,
  MacroToRun) runs the second macro only if the first returns
  non-zero. (An IfThenElse macro also exists.)

Topic pages

You can include as many topic pages in a Help file as you want, but
each must be on its own page in the rich text file. Each topic
requires at least one footnote, the topic identifier designated by
the poundal (#).

Insert a page break after you enter the text you want to display in
the topic window. From the WordPerfect menu, choose Insert⇨
Page Break; in Microsoft Word, choose Insert⇨Break, and then
select the Page Break radio button and click OK. In both editors,
you can insert the page break by pressing Ctrl+Enter.

Generally, a topic page has a headline on it in larger type than the
body text. Common practice is to place the footnote identifiers
just before the headline, but placement is flexible. Be consistent,
because you refer to these footnotes throughout the course of
your project.

See also "Topic Files" in this part.

Help Workshop Help File

The Windows Help system is a very mature and stable environment, and its features have grown to meet the needs of developers over the years. The system has far more features than I can cover in a single chapter, but it contains one of the best examples of Help that one can find, as expected. Studying the construction of the Help Workshop's own Help file can give you some ideas of how to build your own.

Start with the "Training Cards" item on the Help menu for step-by-step instructions on many of the tasks involved in building a Help project. The subitems on this menu item change, depending on what you have on the screen. With a blank Help Workshop, the training card walks you through the steps of creating a project file. After you create the project, check it again, and you see that the subitems have changed to "Adding Topic Files," "Adding Bitmap Locations," and "Adding Windows."

Choose Help⇨Help Topics, and jump off into almost any of the listings; you can find much help on Help. Use this chapter of this book to start building your Help project, but don't hesitate to jump into the Workshop's Help file to get detailed information.

Testing Help Files

As with any programming project, you need to test your Help file frequently. The Help Workshop is not as easy as the Visual C++ environment is in pointing you to errors. The Help Workshop simply tells you an error exists; you have to find it.

Test the Help project by pressing the Test button (the one with a "?" icon on it). This button is the only way to interactively test the project. The Test menu offers some options, but none of them mimic this button (but some come close).

From the Test menu, you have four options.

- ✦ **Contents File:** Tests the integrity of the contents file. If you opt to test the jumps in the contents file, the Workshop performs all the jumps that the file contains. (This process passes quickly, though.)

- ✦ **Close All Help:** Often in a large project you may have several Help files open in the Workshop in test mode. This option closes all the Help files and starts you off with a clean slate. (Close All Help does not close any project files.)

- ✦ **Send a Macro:** Enables you to test a macro by sending it to the Help file. The Help file must be open (for example, running under test mode), and the macro must be one that is contained in the Help file.

✦ **WinHelp API:** Sends a command to WinHelp for the selected Help file. Select the command to send from the combo box. For example, selecting the HELP CONTENTS message opens the selected Help file at the contents topic.

Help Author Mode

The Help Author mode helps troubleshoot and build Help projects. This mode changes the behavior of WinHelp — its error messages are more descriptive, and it gives more information about topics and hotspots.

You can toggle Help Author mode on or off by choosing File⇨ Help Author. Just before the most recent file list is an item titled "Help Author." If this item has a check mark next to it, Help Author mode is on. If not, select this item to turn the mode on. Notice that any Help file already running is not affected until you close and restart that Help file. The title bar then shows "Help Author On."

In Help Author mode, numbers that indicate the relative position in the rich text file replace the title bar text. You can go directly to another topic by pressing Ctrl+Shift+J and then entering its relative number.

Pressing Ctrl+Shift+Home takes you to the first topic in the file, and Ctrl+Shift+End takes you to the last item. Ctrl+Shift+Left Arrow and Ctrl+Shift+Right Arrow steps you forward or backward, respectively, through the topics.

Two new items now are available in the Topic Information window (summoned when you right-click on a topic window and select Topic Information). These items show you the actual topic ID and the file that contains the topic.

Finally, the Help Workshop adds a new item — Ask On Hotspots — to the Topic Information menu. This option is a toggle, so select it once to turn it on, select it again to turn it off. When you click on a hotspot with this option on, WinHelp displays a dialog box. This dialog box shows the hidden text of the hotspot item and gives you the option of executing the jump or macro or staying in the current topic.

Topic Files

Topic files are the rich text files the Help Workshop uses to create the text for your Help file. Strangely, the Help Workshop provides no editor for writing topic files. To write or edit topic files, you need a rich text editor that can handle footnotes and hidden text, such as Microsoft Word or WordPerfect. WordPad, while it is a rich text editor, isn't up to the task.

If you are using Word 97, be sure you have at least Version 4.03 of the Help Workshop. Earlier versions cannot compile rich text files prepared by Word 97. The latest version is available as a free download from Microsoft's Web site.

Microsoft Word

One of the tasks Microsoft Word does well is handling Help topic files. This accomplishment is to be expected. The RICHED32.DLL that comes with Windows has some quirks in it that were intended to support early versions of Word and which will give you problems if you try to use it for your own rich text editor. (Don't bother complaining to Microsoft about the quirks; I did, and was told basically "If it's a problem, don't use it.")

If you plan to use the Dialog Box Help Editor, you need Word.

Here are some of the Word features you need to use in preparing topic files and how to access them:

- ✦ **Hidden Text:** Turn this feature on for viewing hotspots and other Help file formats. Click on the paragraph mark on the Standard toolbar.

- ✦ **Footnotes:** You need to turn on the footnote view because you access many of the Help functions through footnotes. Choose View➪Footnotes.

- ✦ **Text modes:** Use these to select text formatting modes such as underline, strikeout, and hidden text. Access them by choosing Format➪Fonts and then selecting the proper boxes in the Effects section.

You may find it handy to set up a custom toolbar. Choose Tools➪Customize➪New, and then follow the procedures for defining a toolbar.

WordPerfect

Microsoft Word is the preferred editor for topic files, but WordPerfect works — with a little extra effort. My version of WordPerfect is 6.1, and later versions may handle rich text files better.

If you use WordPerfect and also have Word 97, don't even bother to call up a topic file in WordPerfect after Word 97 has edited it. Some of the new coding in Word 97's rich text files causes you to get nothing but a blank screen in WordPerfect.

Some of the features you need to have in WordPerfect and how to access them include:

✦ **Hidden Text:** Turn on this feature. Hotspots in topic files are in hidden text, and you need to see them. Choose View⇨Hidden Text and make sure it has a check mark next to it.

✦ **Text Modes:** Use this to select formatting such as underline, hidden, or strikeout. Choose Format⇨Font, and select the appropriate check box(es) in the Appearance section.

✦ **Footnotes:** WordPerfect did not provide any way to display footnotes — at least up to Version 6.1. Choose Insert⇨Footnote, and then choose Create or Edit as appropriate. This is a major disadvantage of WordPerfect because you frequently need to refer to the footnotes. Having the footnotes constantly displayed, as in Word, is a nice touch.

With WordPerfect, the WYSIWYG (what you see is what you get) display is better than in Word, but you may find the footnote symbols difficult to read.

Visual C++ Help Tools

The Help Workshop is, of course, the primary Help tool that the Developers Workshop provides, but you may find a couple of other tools handy and necessary. These tools are the "Segmented Hypergraphics Editor" and the "Dialog Box Help Editor."

If you've installed the Help Workshop from a package outside the Developers Studio (say, from the upgrade from Microsoft's Web site), you see these two tools as separate items on the Start Menu. Otherwise, you see them only as menu items on the Help Workshop's Tools menu. "Shed" on the menu is the hypergraphics editor.

Segmented Hypergraphics Editor

Another name for the Segmented Hypergraphics Editor is the "Hotspot Editor," but you can just call it *Shed,* for short. It's much easier to remember. A *hypergraphic* is a bitmap that includes hotspots for jumping to Help topics. Shed is the tool you use to create these bitmaps and associate topics with areas in the bitmap.

To use Shed, you first need a hypergraphics (.shg) file, which you can prepare from an ordinary bitmap file (.bmp or .dib) or a metafile (.wmf).

To create a hypergraphics file, follow these steps:

1. Using a graphics program, create the bitmap you want to use for the hypergraphic. Or, using a tool such as Paint Shop Pro, capture the screen area or object (such as a dialog box) you want to provide help for, and save the image as a Windows bitmap.

2. Start Shed, and open the file you just created. You can start editing it immediately as though it were a hypergraphic.

3. Save the file as a hypergraphic by choosing File⇨Save As and selecting .shg as the file type.

You now have a hypergraphic that you can include in your Help file. By defining areas and objects on the graphic (hotspots) and assigning them topic IDs, you can make your Help file jump to other areas or display pop-up windows to explain the object.

To create a hotspot and add a topic ID, follow these steps:

1. Using the left mouse button, drag a box around the area or object you want to define as a hotspot. Release the mouse button. If you make a mistake or need to redraw the area, just select it with the mouse and hit the Delete key.

2. Double-click the area you just defined. An Attributes dialog box appears.

3. In the Binding section, put the topic ID in the Context String field. Select the action in the type field (select pop-up window, jump to another window, or run a macro), and select whether you want the box around the defined area to be visible or invisible when it displays in the Help window.

4. Give the hotspot a name in the Hotspot ID box. (This name is used only for reference, so make the hotspot name meaningful to yourself.)

5. If you need to adjust the rectangle you drew, you can change the values in the Bounding Box field.

6. Click OK to close the dialog box.

Include this graphic in your Help file. (See the section "Graphics" under "Editing Help Files.") When you compile and run your Help file, left-click on the area of the graphic you defined to make sure the proper action occurs.

Dialog Box Help Editor

The Dialog Box Help Editor is designed to assist you in creating context-sensitive help for dialog boxes in your application. You need to be aware of two caveats regarding the DBHE: You cannot use this editor for pre-Windows 95 applications, and you must have Microsoft Word installed to use DBHE.

To use the editor, you need to create a project for it, even if you selected Context Sensitive Help when you created your Visual C++ application. To create the project:

1. Start the Dialog Box Help Editor. The most common method is from the Tools menu of the Help Workshop, but it can run independently of the Workshop.

2. Choose File⇨New Project.

3. Enter the name of the executable module for your application (or library) and the header file to contain the Help IDs. Use the Browse button to locate these if necessary.

4. Give it the name of your topic (rich text) file, or press the New button to have your context help put in a separate file. In the latter case, you are asked to give the file a name. If you create a new file, be sure to add it to the Help project in the Help Workshop.

After you click the OK button, the editor creates your project and displays the available dialog boxes in a combo box in the main toolbar.

You can return to this point at any time simply by reopening the project file from the Dialog Box Help Editor. You are ready to start writing your context help.

1. In the combo box in the main toolbar, select the dialog box for which you want to write context-sensitive help. The selected dialog box appears.

2. Select a control for the topic by clicking the control. The editor starts Microsoft Word and surrounds the control with a red box.

3. Write the text for your topic. (Don't forget the headline.) Notice that the editor has placed a poundal (#) footnote for the topic already. This is a required footnote for all topics, but you can add others at this point.

4. When you finish, choose File⇨Save Project. If you haven't already saved the project file, you need to give it a name.

Part VI

Constants, Arrays, and Variables

The Visual C++ program provides you with a robust set of variable types and data types. This part provides the syntax for using the various C++ data and variable types.

In this part . . .

- ✔ C++ data types
- ✔ Casting variables
- ✔ Constants
- ✔ Declaring and accessing arrays
- ✔ Functions as variables
- ✔ Pointers
- ✔ String handling
- ✔ Variables

Arrays

As in most languages, an array in Visual C++ is a storage area for multiple elements of the same data type. Unlike most languages, however, that's about as far as the definition goes. Neither C nor C++ places many restrictions on arrays, and runtime modules generally don't check the range of an array to make sure you're not trying to access a nonexistent array element.

This isn't necessarily a bad thing, however. Keeping your arrays in order is up to you, the programmer. And you should write your code so that you don't overstep the bounds of the array. In the end, though, it gives you much greater freedom for building and accessing arrays.

Accessing array elements

You can access an array element placing the index of the element in brackets following the array name. For example,

```
int i = MyArray[6];
```

would access the seventh element (the first element is 0) in the array of integers named MyArray.

You can access multidimensional array elements similarly. Just specify the position in each dimension.

```
int i = MyArray[6][2];
```

sets i to the value in the seventh row of the third column of the array.

Remember: The index can be anything that evaluates to an integer — a number, variable, expression or a #define constant.

If you use a noninteger value as the index, some compilers simply cast the value to a whole number (integer), but Visual C++ generates an error.

The C and C++ languages place few restrictions on accessing array elements, and reading nonexistent array elements is possible. For example:

```
int i, MyArray[10];

i = MyArray[17];
```

is perfectly valid and doesn't generate a compile error. In most cases, such expressions don't cause runtime errors, but the resulting value of i doesn't have any meaning. You need to make sure your indexes are within the bounds of the array.

Pointers can also access array elements. The name of the array is nothing more than a pointer to the first element. For example, the code

```
int MyArray[6] = {12, 120, 3, 42, 15, 26, 97};
int i = *(MyArray + 3);
```

returns 42, the value in the fourth element of the array. The asterisk in the expression means "get the value that is stored at this address." Programmers call this technique *de-referencing the pointer*. Note that because an int is 4 bytes, the third element actually begins in the 12th byte of the array, but I added only three to the pointer variable. The compiler makes the adjustment for me, and multiplies my value by the size of the data object.

See also "Declaring pointer variables" and "Pointer arithmetic" in this part.

Declaring arrays

Declare an array in the following format:

Syntax	Example	What It Does
Type Of Array Name Of Array [Number Of Array Elements]	int IntArray [10];	Declares IntArray as an array of ten integers

You can declare an array of any C or C++ data type, or any object you have typed with the typedef statement, or even structures and classes. The language itself places no restraints on the data type of an array. The declaration

```
struct MyStuff
{
    int MyInt;
    char MyChar;
    char* MyCharPointer;
    char MyCharArray[10];
};
struct MyStuff MyStuffArray[20];
```

declares an array of type struct MyStuff with room for 20 structures.

A string in C and C++ is an array of type char. When you declare a string such as

```
char MyString[] = "My String";
```

or

```
char *MyString = "My String";
```

the compiler actually creates an array of type `char` with room for ten characters (the length of `MyString` plus one for the terminating NULL character). The compiler also creates a `char` pointer variable (`MyString`) that points to the first character in the array.

The language also places no restrictions on the number of dimensions in an array. You face practical limits, however. Eventually you'll run out of storage, but that's not because of the C or C++ language restrictions.

To declare a multidimensional array, simply include the number of elements in each dimension enclosed in a separate set of brackets. A two-dimensional array would be declared by the number of rows followed by the number of columns. The following code

```
int ArrayTwo[10][20];
```

declares an array with 10 rows, each containing 20 columns.

Arrays of more than two dimensions aren't common in C and C++ programming, but they are possible. If you use them, remember the total size of the array is the product of the size of each dimension and the size of the element type. The declaration

```
int BigArray [5][6][2][20][10];
```

may not look big, but it declares a five-dimensional array with a total of 12,000 integers. The size of an integer in Visual C++ is 4 bytes, so the total size of the array is 48,000 bytes! Adding another dimension with only two elements would double the size of the array.

Declaring an array with no elements, initializing it, and letting the compiler figure out how many elements exist is possible — and common programming practice. Suppose you have an array of baud rates, such as

```
int BaudRates[] = {300, 600, 1200, 1200, 2400,
    4800, 9600};
```

The preceding code sets up an array of seven integers and places the values in the array. If you later add 19200 and 38400 to the array, you don't need to adjust the value in the brackets. But how does your program know how many elements are in the array? The number of elements is exactly the size of the array divided by the size of the data type — in this case an integer. Just set up a `define` statement such as

```
#define    BAUDRATES    (sizeof (BaudRates) /
    sizeof (int))
```

and then use the define in the program code. For example,

```
for (i = 0; i < BAUDRATES; ++i)
{
    // Do something with BaudRates[i]
}
```

lets you access every element of the array without ever knowing exactly how many elements exist.

Pointers to arrays

Describing a C++ array without bringing up pointers is almost impossible. In fact, in C++, the name of an array is actually a pointer to the first element in the array.

You don't face too many rules in declaring and accessing arrays in Visual C++. Generally, the compiler imposes more restrictions than the language, and the Visual C++ compiler is more liberal than most. This fact gives the programmer some degree of flexibility in coding.

Declaring an array variable

Declare a pointer variable by prefixing its name with an asterisk *. For example,

Syntax	Example	What It Does
* pointerName, arrayName [NumberOfArray Elements];	int *pVar, Array [10];	Declares pVar as a pointer to the first element of a ten-element array named Array.

Because an array variable is actually a pointer to the first element in the array, you can set a pointer variable to an array variable directly. For example,

```
int *pVar, Array[10];
    pVar = Array;
```

is a legal operation.

When you increment (or decrement) a pointer variable, C++ adds (or subtracts) the size of the data element to the original value of the variable. In the above example, pVar is set to point to Array[0]. If you increment the variable by ++pVar (the same as pVar+1), it then points to Array[1]. The size of an integer, whether 2 bytes (as in DOS) or 4 bytes (as in Windows 9x), doesn't matter. The compiler sets the size of the data element, and the runtime code then adds that size when the variable is incremented.

See also "Declaring pointer variables" and "Pointer arithmetic" in this part for more on pointers.

Accessing a subset of a large array

In Visual C++, you can access a subset of a large array. Suppose you have an array with 100 elements that contains the set of all integers from 1 to 100. You can define a pointer variable and set it to an address within the table. For example,

```
int OneHundred[100];
int *Sixties, i;

    for (i = 0; i < 100; ++i)
    OneHundred[i] = i;
    Sixties = OneHundred[60];
    i = Sixties[3];
```

defines a set of integers from 0 to 99 and then sets a pointer variable (*Sixties) to point to the 61st element of the array. Then, retrieving the value of Sixties[3] is the same as retrieving OneHundred[63].

C++ Data Types

Visual C++ defines the basic data types in the C++ language and adds some of its own. The language specifies only the minimum sizes for the data types, leaving the specifics to the compiler and operating platform. In the table below, for example, there is no difference between a type int and a type long; the C++ specifications only say that a long cannot be smaller than an int.

Data Type	Category	Size	Use
char	Integral	1 byte	Members of the machine's character set. Usually ASCII.
int	Integral	4 bytes	Basic numerical type. Must contain a whole number.
short	Integral	2 bytes	An integer with a size between type char and type int. Must contain a whole number.

Data Type	Category	Size	Use
_int*n*	Integral	Varies	Used to specify the size of an integer variable. The *n* indicates the number of bits in the data type. May be int8, int16, int32, or int64 yielding a 1-, 2-, 4-, or 8-byte integer. Must contain a whole number. Don't use in portable code.
long	Integral	4 bytes	An integer with a size equal to or greater than the size of an int. Must contain a whole number.
float	Floating	4 bytes	Basic numerical type to contain a fractional value, for example, 123.654.
double	Floating	8 bytes	An extended fractional value type that must be at least as large as type float.
long double	Floating	8 bytes	An extended fractional value that must be as large as a double.

All the number data types are signed by default and may contain positive or negative values. The integral types may be qualified by using the signed or unsigned keyword, restricting their usage to a particular set of numbers.

In addition, you can use a type void to indicate an empty set of values. The primary use is to declare functions that return no values. You can't declare an ordinary variable of this type, but you can declare a pointer variable of type void, indicating it may be used to point to any data type. You also can cast an expression to type void.

Casting Variables

Variables are cast when they are declared, but more than occasionally you need to use a variable of one type as another type. To do this, you must *cast* the variable when it is referenced. The C++ language enforces strict data types, so casting is common practice.

You cast a variable by putting the temporary type declaration in parentheses before the reference to the variable. For example, if var is a variable of type int and contains a value of 35, then var/0.5 returns 17. That syntax is correct for integer arithmetic, but if you need to know the fractional value of the result, you need to cast the variable. The following code

```
(float) var/0.5
```

temporarily makes the runtime module use *var* as a type float and returns 17.5.

One exception to the casting rule is when mixing types char and int. When assigning the value of a char variable to an int variable, the cast is done automatically. Thus,

```
int x;
char c;
    c = 'C';
    x = c;
```

is perfectly valid and sets the value of x to 67, the ASCII value of the character C.

The language specifications don't say anything about casting in the reverse direction, from an int down to a char, but the specifications don't prohibit it either. Visual C++ lets you do this type of automatic cast, but be careful that you don't overflow the size of a type char. The following is perfectly valid in Visual C++:

```
int x;
char c;
    x = 32356;
    c = x;
```

If you expect this code to set c to 32356, you're in for a surprise. The x variable is 32 bits wide and c is only 8 bits wide, so you end up with 100 (a lowercase "d") as the value of c.

Constants

In C++, a constant is like a number; it has an intrinsic value that you can't change. Otherwise, it wouldn't be a constant.

Declare any of the data types as constant by putting the const keyword in front of the declaration. You must initialize a constant at the time of its declaration, and once declared, you cannot change its value.

As with any rule, you can run into exceptions. If the constant is a pointer, you can change the value to point to another object, which then becomes the constant when referenced by the pointer. In the following code

```
int i, j
const int *ip = &i;
```

the compiler would permit you to assign ip=&j later. Also, in this code snippet, you can change the value of i by something like i = 3, but you can't say *ip = 3. You could cast it back to an int to change the values by writing (int) *ip = 3.

Functions as Variables

You can use a function call in place of a variable in an expression or a call to another function if the return value of the function call is the same data type as the variable being replaced. For example, in the following code

```
long f();
int g(long);
void MyFunc ()
{
int i;
long x;
    x = f();
    i = g(x);
}
```

you can substitute i = g(f()) for the second function call, getting rid of the need for the first function call and the variable x.

In their book, *The C Programming Language* (Prentice-Hall), Brian Kernighan and Dennis Ritchie warn that it is possible to write "impenetrable" code by combining operations such as the substitution in the previous example. The code can become so dense that neither you nor anyone else will be able to read or modify it six months later. The important point is to keep the code tight yet still readable, even if you have to add a lot of comments.

Pointers to functions

Pointers to functions can also be members of an array or structure and called as any other function would be called: The declaration must be in the form (*(FunctionName))().

The following code demonstrates using a pointer to a function.

```
int f1();
int f2();
int f3();
int (*(examples[3]))() = {f1, f2, f3};
int i;
    for (i = 0; i < 3; ++i)
    examples[i]();
```

The above code would call f1(), f2(), and f3() in order, the same as if you had called the functions separately.

You cannot increment or decrement a function pointer. Substituting the following code gives a compile error at ++example:

```
int (*(example))();
example = examples[0];
for (i = 0; i < 3; ++i)
{
    example();
    ++example;
}
```

Functions as structure members

To declare a function as a member of a structure, use the same syntax.

```
typedef struct
{
    char    *c;
    int i;
    int (*(example))();
} MYSTRUCT;
```

Then when you declare the structure:

```
MYSTRUCT MyStruct = {"A string", 65, f4};
```

The function would be called as a member of the structure

```
MyStruct.example();
```

Different instances of MYSTRUCT could declare different functions for the member.

Pointer Variables

A pointer variable is not a storage class; it may be declared as a static or automatic variable. A pointer is a data object that contains a memory address. You use it to reference other variables. *Remember:* A pointer is like your mailing address: The address isn't you, but it tells other people where to find you.

Declaring pointer variables

You declare a pointer variable by prefixing its name with an asterisk, as follows:

Syntax	Example	What It Does
`Type *pointerName;`	`int *pInt;`	Declares `pInt` as a pointer to an integer

Dereferencing pointer variables

You can make a pointer point to any variable by prefixing the name of the variable you want to point to with an ampersand (&). For example,

```
int *pInt, i; // Declare pInt as a pointer to
              // an integer and i as an integer
pInt = &i;    // Make pInt hold the address of i
```

is a valid construct. You can *dereference* `pInt` to get the value of `i` by prefixing `pInt` with an asterisk (sometimes called *indirection*). In the above code, `pInt` points to the variable `i`, and you can retrieve `i` by referencing `*pInt`.

In C++, variables are passed to functions by value. Essentially, they are new variables, and the called function may modify the parameter variable without affecting the original variable. This can be a problem when you need the called function to alter the original variable. In this case, you can pass a pointer variable, which contains the address of the original variable. By dereferencing the pointer, the function can modify the variable.

Pointer arithmetic

Pointer arithmetic is no different from ordinary arithmetic except there are only two basic operations — addition and subtraction — and the basic unit of change is the size of the data element referenced by the pointer. You increment a variable simply by adding 1 to it and decrement by subtracting 1. Visual C++ doesn't let you perform other operations such as multiplication or division on pointer variables.

Remember: In pointer arithmetic, you're dealing with memory addresses. If you increment a pointer, you change its value by the size of the data type. In Windows 9x, an integer has a size of four bytes, so incrementing a variable by 1 would add 4 to its value, pointing to the next address where an integer could survive.

You don't need to worry about the size, of course. The compiler figures it all out. If you have an array of structures containing a number of data types, you don't need to add up the sizes. Visual C++ keeps track of the sizes.

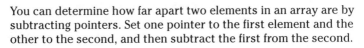

You can determine how far apart two elements in an array are by subtracting pointers. Set one pointer to the first element and the other to the second, and then subtract the first from the second.

The result tells you, in data units, how far apart the two elements are, as shown in the following code:

```
int i;
int *p, *q;
int a[20];
    p = &i;
    p = &a[8];
    q = &a[16];
    i = q - p;
    TRACE1("Difference = %d\n", i;
```

Although the elements are 32 bytes apart, the value of i is 8, which is 32 divided by the size of an integer.

Typecasting pointers

C++ imposes strict typecasting for pointer variables. In the old C, you could have statements such as

```
int *pInt;
char *szChar = "Hello";
pInt = szChar;
```

and the compiler wouldn't complain because both variables are pointers. C++, however, doesn't go for that. One is a pointer to type int and the other to type char. The compiler won't let you assign one pointer to another of a different type unless you cast one to the other. C++ will allow

```
pInt = (int *) szChar;
```

and you often need to do this sort of casting in C++. For example, in handling the scroll message for a slider control, the variable passed to the message handler is a pointer to a scroll bar. To test whether the message came from your slider, you must cast the passed variable to type CSliderCtrl*.

You also need pointers when you allocate global memory using the new operator as in

```
int *pInt = new int;
```

The framework allocates space for an integer, but the only way you can set or retrieve the value is through the pointer.

String Handling

In C++, a string is just an array of type char. When you declare the array, its maximum length is fixed. You must make sure that any changes in the string don't overrun the array bounds. Visual C++ (actually, the Microsoft Foundation Class library) provides a CString class that makes string handling in C++ as easy as in BASIC.

CString contains a number of member functions that take care of the details of string handling, relieving the programmer of having to include code to manipulate the string. At some time in your C++ programming experience, you may find yourself handling strings, and you may realize that any help is welcome. The following table lists some of the more useful member functions:

Member	C++ Equivalent	Use
GetLength	strlen ()	Returns the number of characters in the string
IsEmpty	!strlen()	Returns true if the string is empty
GetAt	string[index]	Returns the character at a given position
SetAt	string[index]=c	Sets the character at a given position
Mid	None	Extracts the middle of a string (similar to BASIC MID$)
Left	None	Extracts the left part of a string (similar to BASIC LEFT$)
Right	None	Extracts the right part of a string (similar to BASIC RIGHT$)
MakeUpper	_strupr()	Converts the string to all uppercase
MakeLower	_strlwr()	Converts the string to all lowercase
MakeReverse	None	Reverses the character sequence
Format	sprintf()	Formats the string
TrimLeft	None	Strips leading white space from the string
TrimRight	None	Strips trailing white space from the string
Find	strchr() or strstr()	Finds a character or substring within the string
ReverseFind	strrchr() or strrstr()	Finds the last occurrence of a character or substring in the string
FindOneOf	strtok()	Finds the first match in the string of a character in a set

Variables

The C++ language specification lists four storage classes for variables: *auto, static, extern,* and *register.*

Auto variables (usually referred to as *automatic* by programmers) are created dynamically, usually on the stack, each time a function or block executes and are destroyed when the function or block terminates. The value of an automatic variable is lost between calls to a function.

Static variables are created in a memory area, usually the program's data block, where they stay for the life of the program.

Register variables are the same as auto variables, but the declaration hints to the compiler that it will be used a lot and should be stored in a CPU register. Declaring a variable of register class is wishful thinking; the compiler usually ignores the declaration and treats the variable as auto. If your code contains a pointer to a register variable, the compiler treats the variable as auto by default.

Extern is used to declare a variable without actually setting aside any storage space. You must declare the variable without the `extern` storage class in one of the program's modules.

Automatic variables

An automatic variable is created when the block in which it is declared executes and destroyed when the block goes out of scope (terminates). Its value must be reinitialized each time the block is executed.

In C++, you can declare variables at almost any point, even within conditional blocks or loops. Variables can be accessed only within the block in which they are declared. In the following code, for example,

```
int Function ()
{
int i;
    //Some program code
    while (/* Some condition */)
    {
        int j;
        // Some conditional code
    }
// Additional program code
}
```

the variable i may be referenced anywhere within the function. The variable j, however, may only be referenced within the while loop; it is destroyed when the loop terminates.

Static variables

Declare a static variable by prefixing its declaration with the keyword static. A static variable and its value are retained for the duration of the program.

If a static variable is declared within a function, it can be referenced only within that function, and you can have static variables with the same name in different functions.

Static variables are useful when you need to retain the value of a variable between function calls, such as with a counter variable.

Part VII

Decision-Making Statements

Decision making imparts power to a program and really distinguishes a computer from a simple calculating device. C++ provides the programmer with four powerful statements for controlling program flow: if, while, for, and switch. This chapter goes over the various constructs and how to use them.

In this part . . .

- ✓ For **loops**
- ✓ If **statements**
- ✓ **Labels**
- ✓ **Nested loops**
- ✓ Switch **statements**
- ✓ While **loops**

For Loops

The for loop is a special form that incorporates its own initialization, modification, and test code within the declaration itself.

The declaration of a for loop includes three elements, each separated by a semicolon.

```
for (initializing code; test code; modifying code)
```

In a for loop, the initializing code always executes *once,* before the program enters the loop. The test code executes each time the program enters the loop, including the first time; the loop code executes if and only if this expression is nonzero. The modifying code executes each time the loop ends, after all the statements in the loop execute. You can easily rebuild the following code into a for loop.

```
i = 0
Loop:
if (i >= 3)
    goto LoopExit;
    statement1;
    statement2;
    ...
    i = i + 1;
    goto Loop;
LoopExit:
// Rest of program.
```

Putting all the code into a for loop looks like this:

```
for (i = 0; i < 3; i = i + 1)
{
    statement1;
    statement2;
    ...
}
```

The execution sequence goes like this:

1. The initializing code executes and i is set to *0.* This is the only time this statement executes.

2. The test code executes to see if i is less than 3. If it is not, the loop finishes, even if this is the first iteration of the loop.

3. The statements between the braces execute.

4. The modifying code executes and i is incremented. (You can use C shorthand here and write ++i, i++, or i += 1.)

See also "Increment and Decrement Operators" in Part IX.

5. Go to Step 2.

You can omit any or all of the expressions in the for statement, but you must leave the semicolons. Suppose the test variable i initializes before the for statement and you don't want to initialize it again, the code looks like this:

```
for ( ; i < 3; ++i)
```

The initializing and modifying code may contain multiple statements, each separated by a comma. The test code may be a compound expression.

```
for (i = 0, j = 10; (i < j) && (j > 5); ++i, −j)
```

This statement initializes i to 0 and j to 10, and tests whether i is less than j *and* whether j is greater than 5. On each loop, i is incremented and j is decremented. (In case you're wondering, this loop terminates when both i and j reach 5.)

The following bubble sort routine illustrates the power of a for loop. The bubble sort isn't terribly efficient or fast, but it does require very little coding and can be implemented quickly. It gets its name from the fact that the higher value data elements tend to sink (lead bubbles?) to the bottom of the array as the algorithm progresses.

```
#define    FOREVER    for(;;)

void Bubble (int Nums[], int elems)
{
int        j, sorts, temp;

    FOREVER
    {
        for (j = 0, sorts = 0; j < elems - 1; ++j)
        {
            if (Nums[j] > Nums[j+1])
            {
                temp = Nums[j+1];
                Nums[j+1] = Nums[j];
                Nums[j] = temp;
                ++sorts;
            }
        }
        if (!sorts)
            break;
    }
}
```

See also "Forever Loops" and "Nested loops" in this part.

Notice that the code executes the outer loop elem times, but the iterations of the inner loop go down by one each time the outer loop executes. The sorts variable keeps track of the number of

transpositions the loop has made, and when the array is fully
sorted (sorts is 0), the break statement causes the outer loop
(the FOREVER loop) to exit.

Forever Loops

Programmers use the term, but there's really no such thing as a
forever loop in C++. This loop is constructed from one of the
loop statements (such as for or while). You use it when you
want to repeat code until some external condition happens —
perhaps the user enters a line from the console that signals an end
to the program or loop.

Create a forever loop by using a controlling expression that
always evaluates to nonzero. In the case of the for loop, you can
just leave the expression empty.

```
while (1)
```

or

```
for (;;)
```

Be sure not to put a semicolon after either of these statements or
the program will never get to the following code. In that case you
would have an *infinite* loop. Definitely a bummer.

Suppose you want to continue processing user input until the user
types **bye**. The following snippet of code does just that.

```
main (int argc, char *argv[])
{
char UserInput[_MAX_PATH];
    for (;;)                    // or while (1)
    {
        cout << "Your input? "
        cin >> UserInput
        if (!strcmp (UserInput, "bye"))
            break;
        // Do something with the user input
    }
}
```

Defining a forever control statement and using it in place of the
control statement is common. This action has the added benefit of
making forever loops stand out when debugging the code.

```
#define    FOREVER    for (;;)
```

or

```
#define    FOREVER    while (1)
```

Your loop now becomes

```
FOREVER
{
// Do something code
}
```

If Statements

All high-level computer languages provide some form of conditional statement, and C++ is no exception. The if statement is the basic conditional construct, and it is a very rare program that does not use the if statement somewhere in the code.

Simple if statements

Declaring an if statement is straightforward. Use the keyword if (all C++ keywords are in lowercase) followed by the control expression in parentheses. Next, add the statement to be performed when expression evaluates to nonzero.

You can write the entire construct on one line.

```
if (expression) statement;
```

but most programmers prefer to put the statement on a separate line and indent it four spaces.

```
if (expression)
    statement;
```

The indent signals the reader that the statement depends on the line before it and makes the code more readable. When you have multiple statements following the if expression, the indent becomes even more important.

The expression may be a function call or a compound expression — in fact, anything that can be evaluated as zero or nonzero. If you want the statement to execute because the expression is zero, you can use the not operator, indicated by an exclamation mark (!) in C++.

```
if (!expression)
    statement;
```

The preceding construct reverses the sense of the conditional, and the statement executes if and only if expression evaluates to zero.

To include multiple statements, put them inside curly braces, like this { and }. For example,

```
if (expression)
{
    statement1;
    statement2;
        . . .
}
```

Notice the line containing the if *does not* have a semicolon. A
semicolon would terminate the condition statement, and the block
inside the braces would become an ordinary block of statements.
You get so used to adding a semicolon at the end of each line that
this is a common — and very nasty — programming error.

Many programmers try to avoid this trap by placing the opening
brace on the same line as the conditional expression similar to the
following. The choice is a matter of preference. Placing the
opening brace on a separate line makes the code more readable,
but the compiler doesn't care.

```
if (expression) {
    statement1;
    statement2;
}
```

You can declare variables within the braces, but only statements
inside the braces can use them.

```
if (expression)
{
    char ch;
    int i;

    statement1;
    statement2;
    ...
}
```

When the conditional block exits, the variables cease to exist, and
the program can't use them.

If-else statement

The statement or statements following an if expression execute
only if the expression evaluates to nonzero. You may provide
alternate statements by placing them after an else keyword. An
if . . . else statement, in its simplest form, looks like this:

```
if (expression)
    statement1;
else
    statement2;
```

If the expression evaluates to nonzero, `statement-1` executes. If the expression evaluates to zero, `statement-2` executes.

Note the placement of the semicolons. No semicolons appear on the lines containing the `if` and `else` keywords, but each of the statements must end with a semicolon.

You can include multiple statements after the `else` keyword by enclosing them in curly braces, as shown in the following code.

```
if (expression)
{
    statement1;
    statement2;
    statement3;
}
else
{
    statement4;
    statement5;
    statement6;
}
```

Many programmers prefer to include the braces even if there is only one statement. The braces isolate the code for debugging, and if programmers later add additional statements, the braces are already in place, eliminating a source of program error.

See also "Switch Statements" in this part.

Multiple else conditions

You can stack `else` conditionals by placing alternate `if` statements after each `else`. In the following example, each `else` except the last one *must* have its own `if` statement. The `if` is optional on the last `else` statement.

```
if (conditional-expression-1)
{
    statement1;
    statement2;
}
else if (conditional_expression2)
{
    statement3;
    statement4;
}
else if (conditional_expression3)
{
    statement5;
    statement6;
}
else
```

(continued)

(continued)

```
{
    statement7;
    statement8;
}
```

This sample declares four blocks of code, only one of which executes, regardless of the value of the conditional statements. If `conditional_expression1` is nonzero, the block following it executes and the rest of the code is ignored.

Similarly, the second block executes only if `conditional_statement1` is zero and `conditional_statement2` is nonzero. The third block executes only if the first two conditionals are zero and `conditional_expression3` is nonzero.

Finally, the last block executes if and only if all the conditionals are nonzero.

Remember: The important point here is that only one block of code executes, even if more than one conditional statement evaluates to nonzero.

A lengthy `if . . . then . . . else` series may be exhausting to debug. If the test object is an integral type (`char`, `int`, or `long`), consider using the `switch` construction.

See also "Switch Statements" in this part.

Labels

Declare a label by typing its name and adding a colon at the end.

Labels are extremely rare in C++ programming, but they are a part of the specification for the original C language. In fact, most textbooks on C and C++ totally ignore labels.

Labels are almost always used with the `goto` statement, which itself is a rare bird in C++

```
goto MyLabel;
// Some code that will not be executed.
MyLabel:
```

This construct may be useful as a debugging tool to temporarily jump over some code. Otherwise, the `goto` label combination has little use. Although some programmers use the combination to break out of a deeply nested loop, you rarely find programming constructs in C++ that can't be accommodated by using other statements.

Loops

Repetitive code is common in programming, and you often find yourself writing lines of code that are similar but may differ only in the value of a variable. Most languages, including C++, provide some means of looping to reduce the amount of code and program size. Tighter code means shorter programs, which load and run faster.

C++ provides two powerful loop statements: the while loop (including the special form do-while) and the for loop.

See also "For Loops," "Forever Loops," and "While Loops" in this part.

Exiting loops

You can terminate loops prematurely by using the break statement. Normally, loops terminate themselves when the controlling expression is 0, but a break is the only method of terminating a *forever* loop (other than exiting the program).

See also "Forever Loops" in this part.

In the following code, the loop continues normally unless the conditional expression (perhaps the result of one of the statements) is nonzero.

```
for (i = 0; i < 3; ++i)
{
    statement1;
    statement2;
    if (conditional_expression)
        break;
}
```

You also can abort a loop prematurely without exiting it using the continue statement:

```
for (i = 0; i < 3; ++i)
{
    statement1;
    if (conditional_expression)
        continue;
    statement2;
}
```

In this case, statement1 would execute; then if conditional_expression is true, statement2 would not execute and the loop would start from the top.

Nested loops

The code within a loop statement may itself contain another loop. The C++ language puts no limits on the number of levels you may nest loops.

To nest a loop within another loop, simply write the code for the loop as though it were not within the other loop. A nested loop may be a while or for loop, regardless of the type of the outer loop.

Suppose, for example, you have a two-dimensional array and you want to initialize all the elements. The following code demonstrates how.

```
int AnArray[20][10];
    for (i = 0; i < 20; ++i)
    {
        for (j = 0; j < 10; ++j)
        {
            AnArray[i][j] = i * 10 + j;
        }
    }
```

When the loop finishes, the array initializes with all the numbers from 0 to 199. Notice that i remains constant while the inner loop executes; i isn't incremented until the inner loop finishes.

Switch Statements

The switch statement is the programmatic equivalent of a radio button group; you can select one of the buttons (conditions) and perform different actions. The switch statement allows you to examine the different values an integer expression can have and execute different code depending on the value.

In the following snippet, the xs are integer constants.

```
switch (expression)
{
    case x1:
        // Some code based on x1
        break;
    case x2:
        // Some code based on x2
        break;
    case x3
        // Some code based on another x
        break;
    default:
// Code to execute when none of the
// above conditions is true
        break;
}
```

The switch statement is not a loop; it executes only once. If you need to execute the statement more than once, include it in a for or while loop. The switch statement is a powerful programming tool, but you need to keep some rules in mind when using it:

+ The *expression* must evaluate to an integer value. This means it must be of type char, int, or long. The switch statement doesn't work with floating-point numbers.

+ The value for each case statement must be a constant. You can't use an expression or a variable here. The case object (represented by x1, x2, and x3) can be a constant, a defined value, or anything the compiler recognizes as a constant value.

+ You can have only one constant value for each case statement. You can't specify a range such as 3 through 6; for this you would need separate case statements for 3, 4, 5, and 6, but you can stack them.

  See also "Cases" in this part for an explanation of stacking cases.

+ The set of cases must be included in curly braces.

You *can't* declare variables within a case, but you can declare them immediately after the opening brace. Variables declared within a switch statement can be used only within the curly braces. In this code,

```
switch (expr)
{
int var1;
    case 3:
        int var2;
```

the declaration of var1 is allowable, but the declaration of var2 results in a compile error. When the switch statement gets completed, var1 goes out of scope and is no longer usable.

You also shouldn't include the block of code in a case inside curly braces. Visual C++ is forgiving in this, but other compilers may not like it.

You can include code in curly braces if it is part of another statement such as a for or while loop, or even another switch statement. (Yes, the code in a case may contain another switch statement.)

See also "Default" in this part.

Cases

A switch works like a multiple if . . . then . . . else statement, and the cases are the blocks of code that execute if the condition is true. You can replace the following code:

```
if (i == 1)
{
// statements
}
else if (i == 2)
{
// statements
}
else
{
//statements
}
```

with

```
switch (i)
{
    case 1:
        // statements
    break;
    case 2:
        // statements
    break;
    default:
        // statements
    break;
}
```

Unlike an if-then-else construction, the values in a case statement must be constants and must be of an integral type (char, int, or long). The values should (but don't have to) be the same type as the expression contained in the switch statement itself; a good compiler such as that in Visual C++ promotes them to the same type.

The case constant must be of a single value. Ranges aren't allowable, but you can stack multiple cases to get the same effect. The snippet of code below effectively builds a range case for 3 to 6:

```
case 3:
case 4:
case 5:
case 6:
// Code to execute for cases 3 through 6
break;
```

The cases do not have to be in order. I could have just as easily reversed the order of the cases above or scrambled them. For readability, though, you should arrange them in some logical order.

The break statement is optional; but if you don't include it, the execution falls through to the next case statement. The break causes the switch statement to exit, just as in a loop. In the above example, if I put a break after case 3, the switch statement would end without ever getting to the code. Without it, however, the case falls through to case 4, which falls through to case 5 and to case 6, and the code executes.

Default

The default is a special case and doesn' have to be included in the switch statement. Statements included in the default case execute if the expression doesn't evaluate to any of the cases.

Use the default case even if it only contains a break statement to make the code more readable. A good optimizing compiler such as Visual C++ ignores it anyway if there is no program code.

If you include the default case, it should be the last case in the switch statement. Visual C++ doesn't care where you place the default case, but many compilers give you an error if additional case statements follow. For readability, the default case marks the end of the code if you place the default case last. Don't develop a bad habit; put the default case at the end.

While Loops

The while loop takes on two forms — an ordinary while loop where the conditional statement executes before the loop block, and a do . . . while loop where the conditional statement appears at the end of the block.

You construct the simplest form simply by adding the while keyword and following it by a conditional expression in parentheses:

```
while (conditional_expression)
```

Notice the lack of a semicolon at the end of the statement. The conditional-expression may be a simple expression, a function call, a compound expression, or anything that can be evaluated to either zero or nonzero. Follow the declaration with one or more statements to execute when the expression evaluates to nonzero. If you have more than one statement, enclose the statements in curly braces.

```
while (conditional_expression)
{
    // Statements to execute.
}
```

If the conditional expression is 0 when the loop is entered, none of the statements in the loop execute.

In the do ... while loop, the statements execute at least once before the expression is evaluated:

```
do
{
    // Statements to execute.
} while (conditional_expression);
```

The statements execute before the expression is evaluated for the first time. If it is nonzero, the program returns to the do and repeats the process. Note that in this form, a semicolon *does* belong after the conditional expression; in fact, it's required in this form of the loop.

Part VIII

Classes

A class is really nothing more than a special type of a structure; but the way classes are constructed, derived, and related is important in object-oriented programming. In this part, you go over how classes are used in programming and figure out how to build classes from other classes.

In this part . . .

- ✔ Abstract classes
- ✔ Accessing class members
- ✔ Base classes
- ✔ Constructors
- ✔ Derived classes
- ✔ Destructors
- ✔ Friend classes
- ✔ Functions
- ✔ Inheritance and class families
- ✔ Naming
- ✔ Overloading
- ✔ Structures
- ✔ Virtual classes

Abstract Classes

An *abstract class* is a schematic — an outline from which you can derive a class. Its purpose is to provide a base class you can build upon by deriving new classes. You can't declare an instance of an abstract class, but you can derive your own class from it and declare an instance of that derived class.

Define an abstract class by declaring one or more member functions as virtual, but set the address to NULL. This type of function is called a *pure virtual function,* and you don't have to write the code to implement it. Just declaring it is enough to establish the class as an abstract class. You do, however, have to write the code to implement other functions in the class that are not pure virtual.

When you derive a class from an abstract call, your derived class must override the pure virtual function, and you have to write the code to implement the overridden function, for example:

```
class CTool
{
    public:
        virtual int     ToolType (int type) = 0;
};
```

In the preceding example, you can't declare a variable of the CTool class. Instead, derive a class from it and write the code to override and implement the pure virtual function ToolType().

```
class CHammer : public CTool
{
    public:
    CHammer (int tool) {TypeOfTool = tool;}
    Int     ToolType (){return(TypeOfTool);}
private:
    int     TypeOfTool;
};
```

Now you can declare a CHammer variable, which derives from the base class CTool because the function ToolType() now has a body of code to implement it.

```
#define    ClawHammer   1
    CHammer    MyTool (ClawHammer);
```

Use an abstract class where you intend to define common properties that other classes derived from the abstract class will use. In addition, using such a class can prevent accidentally declaring a class where it would be meaningless without the individual properties.

Class CView is an example of an abstract class that is intended to serve as a base class for other view classes. If you try to create an instance of CView, the compiler gripes with the following error message:

```
'CView' : cannot instantiate abstract class due to
    following members:
'void CView::OnDraw(class CDC *)' : pure virtual
    function was not defined
```

See also "Base Classes" and "Derived Classes" in this part.

Accessing Class Members

C++ provides mechanisms for protecting member variables and functions in a class that may be sensitive to external tampering, either intentional or accidental. Members may be given public, private, or protected access. Each access specifier has different characteristics, as shown in the following table:

C++ Keyword	Access Allowed
public	May be accessed from any function using the class or variable name
private	May be accessed only by member functions of the class and by friends of the class in which it is declared. This access level is the default if you haven't declared any access privilege. Ideally, variables should be included in a private section.
protected	May be accessed by functions that are members of the class, friends of the class in which it is declared, and by member functions or friends of a derived class

See also "Friend Classes" in this part.

Knowing whether a variable or function should be public, private, or protected takes a lot of experience. Even veteran programmers find themselves adjusting the access privileges of class members.

After you declare an access keyword, all members following are of that type unless you declare another access level.

You're not limited to just one block of public, private, or protected declarations. You can declare sections in any order, although it's customary to declare a public section first for the public constructor. You can declare multiple sections of any access. Say you want to keep your member variable declarations separate from your member functions (this is common practice), you can declare access levels in each.

```
class MyClass
{
// Declare function prototypes
public:
    MyClass ();
    ~MyClass ();
    // Other public functions
private:
    // Private functions
protected:
    // Protected functions

// Declare class data members
public:
    // Public data members
private:
    // Private data members
protected:
    // Protected data members
};
```

The private keyword

Private access is the default access level for all class members if you haven't declared an access specifier.

Only member functions of the class and friend classes may access class members that you have declared private.

In the following code, the constructor initializes TypeOfTool. You find no member functions to change it and no friend classes; so once TypeOfTool initializes, you can't modify it.

```
class CHammer : public CTool
{
public:
    CHammer (int tool) {TypeOfTool = tool;}
    int ToolType (){return (TypeOfTool)
private:
    int TypeOfTool;
};
```

If you try to change TypeOfTool as in the following code, you get a compile error telling you that the variable is "not accessible." In fact, you can't even retrieve the value of TypeOfTool unless you use the member function ToolType().

```
CHammer MyTool (Hammer);
    MyTool.TypeOfTool = Wrench;
```

If you declare a function private, it can be called only by other member functions of the class (or by functions in friend classes).

Generally, C++ practice is to declare all data members of a class `private` and then use `public` or `protected` functions to access them.

For quick access to member variables, you may declare functions to access them `inline`; the compiler substitutes the proper code in the program rather than calling a function.

See also "Inline" in the "Functions" section.

The protected keyword

Members with the `protected` specifier are semiprivate. These members are private to any functions outside the class. However, they are public to statements in a derived class, to friends of the class, and to friends of derived classes. This special access level lets you hide class members from the outside world, yet still be able to access them in derived classes.

In the following example, `TypeOfTool` is a protected member of the base class `CTool`, but it is accessed from a derived class as if it were a local member:

```
class CTool
{
public:
    virtual int     ToolType (int type) = 0;
protected:
    int      TypeOfTool;
};
class CHammer : public CTool
{
public:
    CHammer (int tool) {TypeOfTool = tool;}
    int      ToolType (){return (TypeOfTool);}
};
```

The `TypeOfTool` variable is set when an object of class `CHammer` is created and there's no way to change the variable. You may retrieve the value *only* by calling the `ToolType()` function in the derived class.

The public keyword

The public-access specifier exposes a class member to any statement inside or outside the class. This level provides no protection at all. You can declare any member object `public`, but you can turn to some good programming practices for guidance.

I don't know of any formal rule, but C++ practice is to use the `public` keyword only for functions. Data members of a class usually are declared `private`. If you need to access data members,

declare a `public` member function to access or modify it. Keeping data private ensures encapulation.

See also "The private keyword" in this section.

Base Classes

C++ allows you to reuse existing code by building new classes from others. Many of the classes in the Microsoft Foundation Class library, which is provided with Visual C++, are intended to be used as building blocks for your own classes.

See also "Inheritance" in this part.

When you use a class as the basis for a new class, the original class becomes the *base* class and the new class is the *derived* class. A base class is the building block for other classes and is at the heart of the concept of reusable components. Use a base class to set up common functions and variables to be used by classes you build from the base class.

You can define a base class when you have two or more classes that are the same except for a few properties. Put the similar properties in one class, and then derive your new classes from this base class. Each new class will have the same properties. You can start with a very general base class, and then derive more specific classes from this class. Any class may serve as a base class.

See also "Derived Classes" in this part.

Suppose you have a class called `CAnimal` that contains variables describing animals in general. To describe domesticated animals as opposed to wild animals, you can build a class based on `CAnimal`.

```
class CDomestic : public CAnimal
{
    // Functions and variables to describe
    // domesticated animals
};
```

The new class is the derived class and inherits all the properties of `CAnimal`, which becomes the base class. Similarly, you could derive a `CWild` class that would inherit the properties of `CAnimal`, but you could give it a different set of properties to differentiate it from domesticated animals.

To go even further, you could then derive classes `CDog` and `CCat` from `CDomestic`, as shown in the following code:

```
class CDog : public CDomestic
{
    CDog (char *breed);
    // Statements and variables describing dogs
};
class CCat : public CDomestic
{
    CCat (char *breed);
    // Statements and variables describing cats
};
```

When you declare instances of CDog and CCat,

```
CDog    MyDog("Pomeranian");
CCat    MyCat("Persian");
```

MyDog would have all the properties of CDog, Cdomestic, and CAnimal, but *not* CCat. Similarly, MyCat would have the properties of CCat, Cdomestic, and CAnimal, but not CDog.

The sequence builds down from the most generic to the most specific. You can see how using base classes to hold common elements simplifies your programming. You can reuse common code simply by making it part of a derived class.

Class Variables

A *variable* is a unit of data that has a name that is unique within its scope. The variable can be as small as a single bit in a bit field or as large as the program's largest data object. You can overload functions and operators, but you can't overload a variable.

In a class, declare variables private unless you have a compelling need to give them a more open access specifier. This tactic protects variables from being accidentally changed or given invalid values. Instead, use public or protected functions to set and retrieve them.

You may ask what the difference is. You still can get and set the variables at will even if it is through the functions. Look at the following situation:

```
class MyClass
{
public:
    MyClass ();
    Int     AnArray[4];
}
void MyFunction ()
{
int count;
MyClass AnInstance;
```

(continued)

(continued)

```
    for (count = 1; count < 5; ++count)
        AnInstance.AnArray[count] = count;
}
```

You're setting only four items in the array, but you've mistakenly assumed the array starts at index 1. When count reaches 4, you actually are setting the fifth (and nonexistent) item in the array. You'll accidentally write over something else or, worse, get an exception thrown at you.

Now, suppose you make AnArray private and allow access only through a public function with this code:

```
int MyClass::SetArray (int index, int value)
{
    if ((index > 3) || (index < 0))
        return (-1);
    AnArray[index] = value;
    return (0);
}
```

You've protected yourself against that sort of error and given the calling function a method of checking for errors by returning 0 for success or –1 for an out-of-range index.

Naming

A variable name must be unique *within its scope.* You can have variables of the same name in different functions, but be careful in naming global variables and those with limited scope. When referencing a variable, the compiler always selects the variable with the smallest scope. In the following snippet of code, all the declarations of count are permitted, but if you write code this way, you may only confuse yourself:

```
int count;          // Declared globally
void MyFunction ()
{
int count;          // Declared within the function.
    if (<Some true expression>)
    {
    int count;
        // Code that initializes count
    }
    printf ("count = %d", count)
}
```

The preceding code is perfectly legal, and the compiler won't object a bit or even issue a warning. But when you run this code, you may be surprised to find that count used for the printf statement never initialized.

The compiler uses the definition with the smallest scope possible, so within the conditional statement it uses the definition after the opening brace of the condition. That count initialized. But when you get out of the conditional, that definition of count is out of scope and its value is lost. Therefore, the compiler uses the definition within the function for the printf statement, but that variable was never given a value! To make things worse, outside the function, the compiler uses the global definition of count.

This scenario should convince you to make your variable names unique, even when C++ doesn't require it.

Static versus automatic

Normally, when you declare a variable within a function, the runtime code reserves stack space to hold it. When the function completes, the stack is adjusted and the variable is destroyed. These are *automatic* variables — they are created and destroyed automatically.

A *static* variable is allocated storage at runtime and retains its value for the duration of the program unless you change it. If you set the value during one function call, it has the same value when the function is called again. Static variables are handy for counters and flags.

```
void MyFunction ()
{
static bool first = true;
static int counter = 0;

    if (first == true)
    {
        // Do something for the first call
        // to the function.
        first = false;
    }
    ++counter;
    TRACE1("Function has been called %d times\n",
    counter;
}
```

Common sense leads you to believe the variables first and counter initialize each time the function is called, but the static keyword changes their behavior. Instead, they get created and initialized when the program runs, and from that point the runtime code ignores the initialization code. When you set first to false, it remains false until you change it. Similarly, counter increments and contains the new value each time the function is called.

You may have static variables with the same name in different functions, and each gets treated as a separate variable. Within a class definition, however, the opposite is true.

Remember: When you declare a class member static, only one copy of it gets created at runtime, regardless of how many instances of the class you create. The static member is shared by the class instances, and if one changes it, it is changed for all the instances, even those that haven't been created yet. This is true for static variables and functions.

Constructors

In C++, every class must have a function known as a *constructor*. If you don't declare a constructor, the compiler generates a default function.

Constructors set up the basic structure of the class object and initialize any variables within the class instance. The language specification contains a number of tasks the constructor may be called upon to do, but the compiler takes care of that for you. Generally, you want to use a constructor to initialize variables within your class.

Constructors are not inherited, which means you can't use the constructor for a base class as the constructor for a derived class. Obviously, the base class has no sense of what type of class may be derived from it (it may even have been written by someone else, as in the case of the Microsoft Foundation Class), so the base class can't contain code to initialize derived classes.

When you create a class object, the base class constructor is called first and then the derived class.

Declaring constructors

Declare a constructor function by giving it the same name as the class, but don't give it a type such as int or long. You don't need to declare a constructor — the compiler does it for you. A compiler-generated constructor is essentially is will be an empty function (from a programming standpoint), so if you need to pass any variables to your new class or initialize any data members, you need to declare your own constructor.

In the class definition, prototype the constructor under the public: keyword, but don't give it a data type.

```
class CDog
{
public:
    CDog (<any parameters>);
};
```

If you have a derived class and need to pass some parameters to the base class, you need to do two things. You must declare a constructor and pass the parameters to the base class constructor even if your derived base class doesn't use the parameters. For a class named CDog, the body of a constructor would look like the following code:

```
CDog::CDog (<any parameters>)
{
    // Statements to initialize the class instance.
};
```

To pass parameters to a base class, add a colon after your constructor's name and then a call to the base class constructor as shown in the following code:

```
CDog::CDog (<parameters>) : CDomestic (<param-
    eters>)
```

If the base class itself has a base class, its constructor passes the parameters up the line; you don't need to do it here.

Remember: You can't declare a constructor const or volatile, nor can it be virtual or of storage class static. Finally, a constructor does not return a value, and you can't give it a data type such as int or long. Essentially, you can't declare a constructor as anything but, well, a constructor.

Copy constructors

In most cases, you don't need to do anything with a copy constructor except use it. The compiler automatically generates copy constructors; that's part of the language specification.

When a copy constructor is used, the class's constructor is not called. Obviously, the class already is constructed, and calling the constructor more than once can alter member variables that have been changed.

To use a copy constructor, place an ampersand after the type declaration. Copy constructors must be initialized at the time they are used, as shown in the following code:

```
CDog MyDog ("Pomeranian");
CDog& MyDogToo = MyDog;
```

Placing the ampersand before the variable name has the same effect. CDog &MyDogToo = MyDog works just as well, but it can have the side effect of being confused with the address operator, which is also an ampersand.

Notice that the declaration for MyDogToo contains no parameters, whereas the required parameter for CDog is the breed type.

MyDogToo is a copy of MyDog, and all the member functions and variables can be accessed the same as for MyDog.

Using multiple constructors

As with any function in C++, constructors can be overloaded, meaning you can declare more than one of them as long as each declaration differs in the data type returned or in the number or type of parameters.

If you want to be able to create a class instance using different data types, simply declare a constructor for each. In the class definition, add the prototypes, as shown in the following code:

```
class CMyClass
{
public:
    CMyClass (int ivar);
    CMyClass (long lvar);
    CMyClass (char chvar);
};
```

When you write the body of the constructors, the statements should do something based on the type of parameter passed. For example,

```
CMyClass::CMyClass (int ivar)
{
    // Do something with the integer parameter
}
CMyClass::CMyClass (long lvar)
{
    // Do something with the long parameter
}
CMyClass::CMyClass (char chvar)
{
    // Do something with the char parameter
}
```

Now you may declare an instance of CMyClass using an int, long, or char data type.

Declaring a Class

Declare a new class by using the keyword class followed by the name of the new class. Follow the name with an opening brace ({). Declare your class functions and variables, then end the declaration with a closing brace and semicolon (} ;).

In Visual C++, it is common practice to begin a class name with a capital *C* and the letter immediately following in uppercase. For

example, a class describing automobiles can be named
CAutomobile and can be declared as in the following example:

```
class CAutomobile
{
public:
    CAutomobile();      // the constructor
    ~CAutomobile();     // the destructor
protected:
//    declare protected class members here
private:
//    declare private class members here
};
```

If you are deriving a new class from a base class, follow the class
name with a colon, an access specifier for the base class, and the
name of the base class. The declaration for a class CTruck based
on CAutomobile might look like the following:

```
class CTruck : public CAutomobile
```

See also "Base Classes" and "Derived Classes" in this part.

Derived Classes

When you build a new class based on another class, you are
deriving a class. The new class is called the *derived* class, and the
class from which it is derived is called the *base* class. You may
derive a new class from any other class.

See also "Base Classes" in this part.

A derived class inherits the properties of a base class and all the
properties of any classes from which the base class was derived.

The derived class contains all the functions and variables of the
class from which it was derived and will have any additional
variables you add.

To declare a derived class, first name your new class and then add
a colon (:), an access specifier, and the name of the base class.
Assuming YourClass already has been defined, the following
example illustrates how a derived class would be declared:

```
class MyClass : public YourClass
{
public:
    MyClass();
    ~MyClass();
// Additional function and variable definitions.
};
```

The access specifier can be public, protected, or private. The table below shows how the access specifiers act on the base class members:

Specifier	Effect on Base Class
public	None. All base class members retain their original access.
protected	Public members are set to protected; private members are not affected.
private	All members of the base class are set to protected.

The access changes are relative to the derived class and don't actually change in the base class. If you derive yet another class from the base class, you may give the base class a different access specifier.

See also "Accessing Class Members" in this part.

Destructors

C++ provides a method of gracefully destroying a class object. That method, known as a *destructor,* is called when an object is deleted or goes out of scope.

Like a constructor, a destructor must have a data type, and if you don't provide one, the compiler generates a default. Unlike a constructor, however, it can't have arguments.

Declare a destructor by using a tilde (~) and the class name. In the body of the code, include any statements you need to clean up the class construction, such as freeing any memory that may have been allocated.

In the following example, notice that the constructor allocates memory to hold the name of the dog breed, and the destructor frees it. If the memory were not freed, it would be left stranded when the class is destroyed and become what is affectionately known as a *memory leak*. Note also how the class protects itself against accidentally being passed a NULL pointer or a memory allocation error. (In a real class, you would want to write some error handling code if the new operator fails.)

```
class CDog : public CDomestic
{
public:
    CDog (char *breed); // Constructor
    ~CDog ();           // Destructor. No arguments
    char *GetBreed () {return (m_breed);};
private:
    char *m_breed;
};
```

```
CDog::CDog (char *breed)              // The body of
    the constructor
{
    if (breed != NULL)
    {
        m_breed = new char [strlen (breed) + 1];
        if (m_breed != NULL)
            strcpy (m_breed, breed);
    }
    else
        m_breed = NULL;
}
CDog::~CDog ()    //Destructor. Note tilde, no
                  //parameters
{
    if (m_breed != NULL)
        delete [] m_breed;
}
class CDog : public CDomestic
{
public:
    CDog (char *breed); // Constructor
    ~CDog ();              // Destructor. No arguments
    char *GetBreed () {return (m_breed);};
private:
    char *m_breed;
};
```

Friend Classes

Declare a *friend class* by using the friend keyword followed by
the name of the friendly class in the declaration of your class.

I can't find a lot of good things to say about friend classes. They
wreak havoc with many of the tenets of object-oriented programming by exposing elements of the class to unrelated functions.
Sometimes friend classes are useful and even necessary. Just as
you would trust a friend, a class must trust its friends not to do it
harm.

Functions in friend classes have access to all members, data,
and functions, regardless of whether they are declared public,
private, or protected. In the following code, class CDog is
declared a friend of CFireHydrant:

```
class CDog : public CDomestic
{
public:
    CDog (char *breed); // Constructor
    ~CDog ();              // Destructor. No arguments
    char *GetBreed () {return (m_breed);};
```

(continued)

(continued)

```
private:
   char *m_breed;
};
class CFireHydrant
{
public:
   FireHydrant (int height, int plugs, int type)
   {
      m_height = height;
      m_plugs = plugs;
      m_type = type;
   }
   ~FireHydrant ();
private:
   int m_height, m_plugs, m_type;
   friend  CDog;
};
```

Objects of type CDog have access to all the data elements and
functions of CFireHydrant, and the functions in CDog could
modify them. The reverse isn't true, however. Because it's an
unrelated class, CFireHydrant may access only the public
members of CDog.

Functions

Every C++ program must have at least one function named
main(), but in Visual C++, that function is hidden from you. In
using a class library such as the Microsoft Foundation Class, you'll
probably never encounter a main() function. In non-MFC Windows
programming, you'll need a WinMain() or a LibMain() function,
depending upon the type of program you're writing.

In C++, functions must be typed, and they default to int if you
don't give them a data type. You should also declare functions in a
prototype declaration. Make a habit of declaring and prototyping
all functions, including int. Doing so is just good programming
practice, and it helps the compiler to spot program errors. In a
class definition, all functions in a class must be prototyped — a
good habit to get into for functions that are not in a class.

Functions must return a value of the declared type. The only
exception is type void, which is used for functions that do not
return a value; you can't declare a variable of type void, so you
can return a type void.

Inline functions

Calling a function takes time. The compiler must generate code to
reserve stack space for variables, and then the CPU must push the

current program location onto the stack and jump to the function address. This process doesn't take a lot of time, but if you're calling a function thousands of times in loop, it adds up.

Inline functions avoid these steps. Instead of actually calling the function, the compiler replaces each instance of an inline function with the code in the function except, of course, return statements.

Keep inline functions short, however. If you have a lengthy inline function and it appears many times in your program, the size of your executable is going to grow rapidly.

Following is an example of an inline function:

```
inline int CTool::GetToolType ()
{
    return (TypeOfTool);
}
```

Now you can write a statement such as

```
CTool MyTool (1);
int TheTool;
    TheTool = MyTool.GetToolType();
```

And the effective code generated by the compiler is

```
TheTool = TypeOfTool;
```

In essence, this type of construction causes the compiler to override the private keyword and place TypeOfTool directly in the code, yet at the same time maintains the integrity of the class.

Defining the body of a function within the class definition is the same as declaring it inline. Instead of the above function, you could have placed the following in the class definition for the prototype of GetToolType:

```
int GetToolType () {return (TypeOfTool);}
```

Naming functions

You don't need to follow any rules for naming functions other than their names may not be the same as a C++ reserved word. For readability, the name of a function should give a hint as to what it does. For example, it's pretty clear what a function called GetToolType() should return. To reduce typing and to minimize the chance of error, function names should be as short as possible but not so short that you sacrifice clarity. Eventually, you'll develop your own style. If it works for you, stick with it.

The Visual C++ designers developed some conventions for naming functions generated by ClassWizard. If you add a message handler for a menu item, Visual C++ prefixes the name with `On` to indicate an event handler. Next, Visual C++ tacks on some form of the menu item name. Just reading `OnFileNew()` tells you the menu item is an event handler for the `New` item on the `File` menu.

Similarly, if in a dialog box you have an `edit` control named `IDC_BASKET` and you want a message handler for any changes to the control, the ClassWizard generates the name `OnChangeBasket()`.

Case is significant in function names. `OnFileNew()` is not the same as `OnFilenew()`. Using a capital letter for each major component of a naming convention improves readability. `On` indicates an event (message) handler, `File` indicates the File menu, and `New` tells you the component is the New item on the menu.

The wizard names are only suggestions. The Visual C++ naming convention can, and sometimes does, come up with some long function names. You're free to change the name when the suggested-name dialog box pops up.

Overloading functions

Function names do not need to be unique. You can give two functions the same name as long as they differ in the number or type of parameters passed to it. This convention is called *function overloading.*

Suppose in a class named `CDog` you store an integer to indicate the index of a breed of dog and a string to hold the name of the breed. You can declare two functions named `GetBreed()`: one that returns the integer, and the other that copies the name of the breed to a local variable.

```
class CDog
{
public:
    CDog (int iBreed, char *pszBreed);
    int GetBreed (char *pszBreed, int len);
    int GetBreed () {return (m_iBreed);}
private:
    char *m_pszBreed;
    int m_iBreed;
};

CDog::CDog (int iBreed, char *pszBreed)
{
    m_iBreed = iBreed;
    m_pszBreed = new char [strlen (pszBreed) + 1];
    if (m_pszBreed != NULL)
        strcpy (m_pszBreed, pszBreed);
}

int CDog::GetBreed (char *pszBreed, int len)
```

```
{
   if (m_pszBreed != NULL)
   {
      strncpy (pszBreed, m_pszBreed, len - 1);
      return (0);
   }
   return (-1);
}
```

Don't write a function such as the preceding to return a pointer to a member character string. Doing so would expose a private member to access by a nonmember function through the pointer. Instead, return a copy of the string using a length parameter to avoid overwriting the size of the string in the calling function.

The two functions differ in the number parameters, and the compiler and linker can resolve the ambiguous name.

Overloading is common in declaring class constructors, giving you flexibility in creating class objects. The CString class, for example, has seven constructors, each differing in the type of parameter you pass when the class object is created.

Virtual functions

In a derived class, sometimes you will have to override a function contained in a base class to alter its behavior. Normally, function overriding is not a problem until you use a pointer to the derived class. Then the code has a problem distinguishing between the function in the base class and the one in the derived class. When you use a pointer to the class instance, the code will execute the function in the base class.

Check out *Visual C++ 6 For Dummies* (IDG Books Worldwide, Inc.) for a complete description of virtual functions.

You can alter this by declaring the base class function with the keyword virtual. This will force the compiler and runtime code to skip to the derived class function.

The virtual keyword is used in conjunction with any other type specifier. To declare a void function in the base class virtual, write it this way:

```
virtual void MyFunction ();
```

You don't need to declare the derived class function virtual, but it's common practice to do so. It doesn't hurt to declare a function virtual, and it serves as a flag that you are using virtual functions.

Inheritance

The principle of inheritance — the idea of reusing existing programming — probably is one of object-oriented programming's most significant contributions.

Inheritance means you can write generic classes with the intention of never using them directly but instead deriving other classes from them and reusing the generic functions. You don't need to include these functions in your derived class to use them.

To get an idea of inheritance in Visual C++ using the Microsoft Foundation Class, follow these steps:

1. Summon the InfoView index, and type **hierarchy chart.**

2. Select the Class Library Reference and display it. At the top is a class called CObject, which serves as a base class for most MFC classes.

3. Follow the chart lines to see how the classes you use in your programming are derived from this grandfather class.

You'll never see a class object built directly from CObject. Look at the class definition in the file afx.h (don't make any changes). You see that the only constructor is protected — it can be called from only derived classes. Microsoft never intended this class for direct use. Notice, too, that it contains only the basic, low-level functions; you see nothing specific like OnFileOpen().

A derived class inherits all the properties and functions of its base class, so any class derived from CObject has access to its functions. As you work your way down the hierarchy chart, the functions and variables in the classes become more specific.

See also "Derived Classes" in this part for an example of derived classes.

When you derive a class from CDialog, you have to write only the code specific to handling your dialog box — the message handlers for the controls, for example. You can call any public or protected function in CDialog, CWnd, CCmdTarget, and CObject.

The fact that functions for the base classes are already written doesn't mean you're stuck with the code. You can override any public or protected function and write your own code. You can even add to the existing code.

When you're writing classes that can be used as base classes, make the functions you may override *virtual*. If the base class function is not virtual and you access a derived class function through a pointer, the base class function may execute rather than the derived class function. The mechanics of why this happens is beyond the scope of this book. The `virtual` keyword in the base class forces the derived class function to execute.

To override a base class function, you must declare your derived class function exactly like the base class function. The function name, return type, number, and type and order of parameters must be identical. Otherwise, the compiler looks at them as different functions.

`OnInitDialog()` is a common example of overriding and adding to a base class's code. You need to call the base class function to create the controls. Obviously, however, `CDialog` has no sense of what you will do with the controls in your derived class, so it can't initialize them for you. Instead, you override the base class function, call it from your derived function using the syntax `CDialog::OnInitDialog()`, and add your own code to initialize your controls:

```
BOOL CMyDialog::OnInitDialog()
{
    CDialog::OnInitDialog();
    // TODO: Add extra initialization here
    m_basketname = "Basket";
}
```

This function calls the base class function of the same name and then initializes an `edit` control to contain the word `Basket`.

Structures and Unions

Structures, like classes, are named groups of statements used to encapsulate functions and data. Encapsulation is a key feature of the C++ language.

The structure is a concept brought over from the C programming language and is the basis for the class concept in C++. You find only subtle differences between a structure and a class, and in most cases, you can use the `struct` and `class` keywords interchangeably. In fact, if you define a structure in Visual C++ and then examine the Class View pane of the Workshop window, you see that structure listed as a class.

The scope of the keyword `struct` has been redefined in C++. You can move a C structure to a C++ program and use it without modifying it; the reverse isn't necessarily true. For one, C++ structures support function declarations. In C, the only way you can put a function in a structure is to use a pointer to an external function.

Remember: A key difference between a C++ class and a C++ structure is that in a class all the members default to private; in a structure, they default to public. The C language had no concept of access, so all members essentially were public. To maintain portability, C++ carries this across.

A *union* is a special case of a structure. In a structure, a number of data fields are stored one after the other. In a union, declared with the keyword union, these data fields are stored in the same location so it may hold only one data element at a time. The compiler reserves space for the largest member. Unions are handy when you want to store and retrieve different data types from the same location, depending on the state of the program.

Suppose you define a union:

```
union _myunion
{
    int     MyInt;
    char    MyString[32];
    long    MyLong;
} MYUNION;
```

When you declare an instance of MYUNION, the compiler sets aside 32 bytes, the size of the largest member, MyString. You may store an int, a string, or a long in the union, but only one at a time. If you store an int and then later store a string, the string overwrites the previous integer value.

The This Pointer

Every instance of a C++ class contains a special pointer to itself called this. This pointer allows an instance of a class to point to itself without ever knowing its name. Kinda like an amnesiac saying "me."

At times, you will need a pointer to the class instance. For example, the CToolBar::Create() function requires a pointer to the parent window as the parameter. Toolbars generally are created within the mainframe window when it is created, so you can use this to refer to the frame. You don't need to know the class or the variable name of the instance of the frame window.

Virtual Classes

When a class is derived from more than one base class (called *multiple inheritance*), it's possible that somewhere in the hierarchy the base classes are themselves derived from a common ancestor.

In this case, your derived class would inherit more than one copy of the remote ancestor.

I don't see anything wrong with inheriting more than one copy of an ancestor; it won't stop your compile or keep you from running your program. However, it can be annoying. If you reference a function in the common ancestor, there are multiple copies of it, and you have to use the scope resolution operator ": :" to tell the compiler which copy of the function to use. Otherwise the compiler will gripe about an ambiguous function reference.

You can avoid this by declaring the ancestors `virtual` in your base classes. In this case, your derived class inherits only one copy of the common ancestor or ancestors, no matter how many times it is used to derive another class.

The declaration is made at the time you define your derived class simply by adding the keyword `virtual` to the base class name. Suppose `class B` and `class C` are both derived from `class A` and you derive a new class using B and C as the base classes. When you define classes B and C, include the virtual keyword for `class A`.

```
class B : virtual public A
```

and

```
class C : virtual public A
```

Then when you derive your class from B and C, only one copy of `class A` will be inherited.

```
class MyClass : public B, public C
```

You need to do some planning to make this work. You probably won't need to worry about the virtual class keyword until you start building your own base classes. However, you should be aware of the way it works in case you start seeing some odd behavior from the compiler and get error messages about *ambiguous* references.

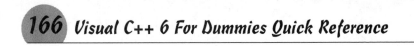

Part IX

Operators

A computer does things by the number, and arithmetic and logical operators are how it expresses the relationship between numbers. In this chapter you go over the various operators, determine how they work, and find out how to use them.

In this part . . .

✔ **Using arithmetic operators**

✔ **Working with assignment operators**

✔ **Manipulating with bit control operators**

✔ **Using increment and decrement operators**

✔ **Looking at logical operators**

✔ **Overloading operators**

✔ **Figuring out operator precedence and the order of evaluation**

✔ **Knowing how to use the** `sizeof` **operator**

Arithmetic Operators

Arithmetic operators enable you to manipulate numbers by adding, subtracting, multiplying, or dividing. Operators are either *unary* or *binary*. A unary operator (either the + or - symbol) needs only one value (called the operand), and the + operator is implied. For example, `42` implies `+42`, and `my_variable` implies `+my_variable`. Binary operators act on two values (operands).

Operator	Rule	Example
+	Unary positive	`i = +42` (implied)
-	Unary negation	`i = -42`
+	Addition	`i = j + 42`
-	Subtraction	`i = j - 42`
/	Division	`i = j / 42`
*	Multiplication	`i = j * 42`
%	Modulo division	`i = j % 42`

The modulo division operator returns the remainder of the division of the two operands and may be performed only on integer values and variables. This operator also is useful for determining when an event occurs. For example, if you want to execute certain code only on every eighth pass of a loop, you can write something like the following:

```
for (i = 1; i < 100; ++i)
{
    if (i % 8)
        // Do something every eighth time
    else
    // Do something else
}
```

Modulo 2 division tells you whether a number (such as a page number) is odd or even.

```
odd = PageNumber % 2;
if (odd)
    // Do something odd
else
    //Do something even
```

Assignment Operators

The equals symbol (=) indicates the assignment operator. The symbol sets the variable that appears to the left of it to the result of the expression appearing to its right. For example, i = 42 sets the value of i to 42.

You can combine the assignment operator with one of the arithmetic or bit-manipulation operators (except for the not operator). For example, where you would write i = i + 42, in C you can write i += 42 and get the same result. The operand to the right of += may be a complex expression.

Operator	C/C++ Example	Usage	Long Equivalent
=	i = x	Set i equal to x	i = x
+=	i += x	Add x to i	i = i + x
-=	i -= x	Subtract x from i	i = i - x
*=	i *= x	Multiply i by x	i = i * x
/=	i /= x	Divide i by x	i = i / x
%=	i %= x	Modulo divide i by x	i = i % x
&=	i &= x	Bitwise AND i and x	i = i & x
|=	i |= x	Bitwise OR i and x	i = i | x
^=	i ^= x	Bitwise XOR i and x	i = i ^ x
<<=	i &= x	Shift i left x bits	i = i << x
>>=	i &= x	Shift i right x bits	i = i >> x

See also "Bit Control Operators" in this part.

C also contains a *conditional assignment* operator, which appears as a question mark. The operator must follow a test expression and must be followed by two expressions separated by a colon. If the test expression is true, then the assignment is made from the expression to the left of the colon. If false, the assignment is made from the expression to the right of the colon. For example,

```
i = test_expr ? true_expr : false_expr;
```

is the same as writing

```
if (test expr)
    i = true_expr;
else
    i = false_expr;
```

Any of the expr expressions may be a value, variable, or a complex equation as long as the result can be assigned to the variable on the left of the equals sign. You can write code that neither you nor anyone else can figure out using C shorthand like this, so use it wisely.

Bit Control Operators

Manipulating bits quickly and efficiently is important, and C++ has an excellent complement of bit operators. Bitwise operators work on corresponding bits in the operands. The table lists the operators and some uses for them follow the table.

Operator	Operation	Result
&	Bitwise AND	1 Only if both bits are 1
|	Bitwise OR	1 If either bit is 1
^	Bitwise XOR	See below
~	Bitwise NOT	1 If original bit was 0
<<	Bitwise left shift	Bits are shifted left
>>	Bitwise right shift	Bits are shifted right

The XOR operator (called *exclusive or* in the world of logic) yields a 1 if and only if the bits are different. Some rules for using the XOR operator are

+ XORing a bit with 0 leaves it in the same state.

+ XORing a bit with 1 toggles it, giving the operator its popular name of the "toggle" operator.

+ XORing a variable with itself sets it to 0.

Increment and Decrement Operators

The assignment operator is used often to increment or decrement a variable, but in C these operations have special notations. To increment a variable, simply precede or follow its name with two plus signs (++). To decrement it, use two minus signs (--). All of the following are equivalent:

+ i = i +1; The value of i is taken, 1 is added to it, and then i is set to the new result.

+ i += 1; 1 is added to the value of i.

+ i++; The value of i is taken, and then 1 is added to it.

+ ++i; 1 is added to the value of i before it is taken.

If the operator precedes the variable name, the operation is performed *before* the variable is used. If the operator follows the name, then the value is used before the operation is performed. For example, if j = 4, then i = --j will set j to 3 and then set i to 3; but i = j-- will set i to 4 and then set j to 3.

You may combine operations on a single line by separating them with a comma.

```
++i, --j;
```

is the same as writing the two statements on separate lines.

Logical Operators

Logical, or relational, operators return only true or false conditions (Boolean values or type `bool` in Visual C++). These operators are key to decision-making operations; a good understanding of them is important in programming.

Operator	Meaning	Result
&&	Logical AND	True only if both operands are non-zero
||	Logical OR	True if either operand is non-zero
!	Logical NOT	True only if the operand is zero
<	Less than	True if the left operand is less than the right operand
>	Greater than	True if the left operand is greater than the right operand
<=	Less than or equal to	True if the left operand is less than or equal to the right operand
>=	Greater than or equal to	True if the left operand is greater than or equal to the right operand
==	Is equal to	True if both operands have the same value and sign
!=	Not equal to	True if the left and right operands have different values

Overloading Operators

It is possible to make the C operators perform other operations depending on the context of the statement. This is called *operator overloading,* and you can see some excellent examples in the `CString` class of MFC.

Unlike function overloading, operator overloading must be done within a class. You can't globally overload an operator. To overload an operator, declare a function in a class definition using the keyword `operator` followed immediately by the operator symbol and a list of parameters in parentheses. The `CString class,` for example, overloads the equals operator, and the declaration looks like the following.

```
CString& operator=(LPCSTR str);
```

See also Part VIII.

The body of the function would contain the code you want to execute when the operator executes

```
CString& ClassName::operator=(LPCSTR str)
{
    // Code to copy str into a CString char[] vari-
    able.
}
```

You then may use the operator to initialize a CString instance.

```
CString string = "This is a CString instance.";
```

 You can have multiple functions for the same operator, but they must differ in the parameters. Any operator other than the following can be overloaded: `sizeof`, the conditional assignment operator (`?`), the scope resolution operator (`::`), the member of operator (`.`), and the indirection operator (`*`).

Precedence and Order of Evaluation

C++ evaluates expressions algebraically from left to right, but some operators take precedence over others. The actual order of operations is complex and takes up a number of pages in the C++ reference manual, detailing such things as the resolution of scope operators and overloaded operators. Generally, however, you'll treat things such as `MyClass::MyVariable` as a single item; the programmers who wrote Visual C++ can't; they must follow the C++ reference.

The following table lists the operators by groups in order of evaluation. Within a group, the order is as listed, but some operators may have equal precedence. For example, the dot (`.`) and pointer (`->`) operators for structures and classes are virtually identical in purpose and precedence. They are evaluated first, along with `this` and the `::` scope resolution operator. The table does not list these primary operators.

Operators	Comments
`() []`	Parentheses first, then subscripts (which may contain parentheses)
`++, --, ~, !`	Increment, decrement, bitwise NOT, logical NOT
`*, /, %`	Multiplication, division, and modulo division
`+, -`	Addition and subtraction
`>>, <<`	Bitwise shifts

Operators	Comments
<, <=, >, >=	Comparison operators
==, !=	Equality tests
&, ^, |	Bitwise AND, bitwise XOR, bitwise OR
&&, ||	Logical AND, logical OR
? :	Conditional assignment

The lowest order of priority is given to the assignment operators. By the time they are needed, the work has been done, and all that remains is to drop the value into the variable. The following all have the same precedence:

```
=  +=  -=  *=  /=  %=  &=  |=  <<=  >>=
```

The Sizeof Operator

The handy `sizeof` operator returns the size, in bytes, of its operand. The operand may be an expression or a type name in parentheses. It may not be used for functions (but you may use it for a pointer to a function), a bit field or an undefined class or structure, a variable or type `void`, or an array with an unspecified dimension.

Be careful of the "expression." It is not evaluated before the `sizeof` operator is applied. The C++ specifications are not clear what is returned in this case, just that it may be applied to an expression "which is not evaluated."

The `sizeof` operator is useful for writing portable code and for finding the number of elements in an array. For example, if you want to compile your program for Windows 3.1 and Windows 9*x*, you may be surprised to find the size of an integer is different. Say you have an initialized array with no particular size, and during the course of your program you want to extract its size, maybe for a loop.

```
int BaudRates[] = {300, 600, 1200, 1200, 2400,
    4800, 9600};
```

How many entries are in this array? Well, you could divide its size by 4, the size of an integer, but that differs on Windows 3.1 and Windows 9*x*. If you use the `sizeof(int)` expression, the value will be correct regardless of the operating system.

```
#define   BAUDRATES      (sizeof (BaudRates) / _
sizeof (int))
```

Part X

Taking Advantage of Windows

Windows 9*x* brought some new and exciting capabilities to the personal computer. Multitasking gave us the capability to run several programs at the same time. Multithreading gave programs the ability to perform several tasks virtually simultaneously. The registry, first introduced in Windows NT, gives us a common database to store program information. Visual C++ allows your application to take advantage of these capabilities.

In this part . . .

- ✔ Using the Windows Registry
- ✔ Giving your program a splash screen
- ✔ Bare basics of threads

Splash Screens

A splash screen is a bitmap that gets displayed when the application is first launched. Splash screens often display the version number of an application and other user information in a graphically appealing format. It gives the user something to look at while your program is initializing, and it gives you a chance to plug yourself or your company.

Many people, particularly old-timers, don't like splash screens. They consider them a waste of code space and computer time. Actually, creating a splash screen takes very little programming effort. (Visual C++ provides a splash screen component.) Also, in an operating system such as Windows 9*x* or Window NT, the computer overhead is almost negligible.

To insert a splash screen into your application:

1. Select Project⇨Add to Project⇨Components and Controls.

2. In the Gallery dialog, select "Splash Screen" and press the Insert button. Visual C++ inserts a splash screen class (`CSplashWnd`) into your application and inserts a call to display it in the `InitInstance()` function of your application class.

3. Compile and run your program; the splash screen appears.

You definitely don't want the default bitmap. The default doesn't really look very good, and it has no information about your application. Use a graphics editor such as Paint Shop Pro or the Microsoft Image Editor to design your own startup screen, add it to your project using the Resource Workshop, and change the resource ID in the `Create()` function of `CSplashWnd`. (The default is `IDB_SPLASH`.)

Remember: There's only one rule to remember when using a splash screen: Have fun with it.

Threads

With multitasking operating systems such as Windows 9*x* and NT, you can load several applications at the same time and programs can execute in the background. Although you can only *use* one program at a time, when one program is busy at a task, you can easily switch over to another and keep working.

An application itself can be doing more than one task at a time through a technique called *threading*. Basically, a thread is another execution point in a program. The thread has its own stack space so it can call functions and use local variables independently of the main thread, and it has access to all the global variables in the program.

Threads don't have to be complicated to be useful. Animation is an example of a thread at work. While you and your program are doing something else, the thread is handling the chore of changing images.

Generally, a task can be offloaded to a thread if the task doesn't require user input. For example, on startup, your program may have to do some time-consuming tasks such as read configuration information or initialize a spell checker.

The Microsoft Foundation Class provides a base class called CWinThread to help you build threads. The following example declares a simple thread:

```
class CHelper : public CWinThread
{
public:
CHelper () {}
~CHelper () {}
    int     Run ();
};
```

In the Run () function, add any tasks you want to perform and then have the thread exit. The following one, for example, writes a couple of messages through a user-defined routine (StatusMessage) and calls a function to initialize a spell-check engine:

```
int CHelper::Run ()
{
    StatusMessage ("Initializing Spell Engine");
    InitializeLex ();
    StatusMessage ("Spell Engine is ready");
    return (0);
}
```

InitializeLex() can be a function in the main application or part of another class, as long as you use the scope resolution operator. The thread is started by a call to

```
phelper=(CHelper*)AfxBeginThread
    (RUNTIME_CLASS(CHelper));
```

You can find entire books about Threads, and the subject is far too involved to cover completely here. Try some small threads with limited scope such as this one, and then gradually make them perform more complicated tasks. You'd be surprised at how they can add some pep to your programs.

Keep these rules in mind when using threads:

✦ A secondary thread should always exit before your main program exits. If the thread has more than a limited lifetime (such as the above example), provide some means of signaling it to stop when your program exits, and wait for it to terminate before letting your program exit.

✦ Don't use a thread where user input or feedback to the user is required. Let your main program code handle any error conditions your thread might send back to it.

✦ Don't use threads for simple tasks just to use them. The overhead involved in running a thread means you should use them as they are intended — for time-consuming or background tasks.

The Windows Registry

Before Windows NT and later Windows 95, programmers used .INI and configuration files to record startup and operating information for their programs. These files worked, but reading them was often cumbersome, and they were prone to user tampering.

With NT came the Registry, a system-controlled database that contains most of the operating system's startup and operating information and in which programmers could store their program's information.

Rather than having to write all the code to decipher the contents of an INI file, you can call Registry functions to set and retrieve program information in the database.

When you create an application using the Visual C++ MFC AppWizard, look in the InitInstance function of your main application program file and you find the following lines:

```
// Change the registry key under which our settings
// are stored.
// You should modify this string to be something
// appropriate
// such as the name of your company or
// organization.
SetRegistryKey(_T("Local AppWizard-Generated
    Applications"));
```

Change the registry key name to something more meaningful to you. Say your program is called Howdy.exe; make it read "The Howdy Company". Compile and run the program.

Two things happen:

+ A registry key gets created for "The Howdy Company", and a subkey for the program "Howdy" gets added below it. Follow these steps to check the entries:

  1. Run regedit.exe. You won't find regedit in any of your Start Menu programs. Wisely, Microsoft keeps it out of public view. To run regedit, select Run from the Start Menu. Type **regedit** in the dialog box, and click the OK button.

  Be careful not to delete or change anything in the registry unless you know what you are doing. Accidentally pressing the Delete key while you have the wrong registry key selected can seriously damage your operating system. Regedit is a useful tool, but it also can be dangerous.

  2. Expand the HKEY_CURRENT_USER key, and then expand the Software entry. There — among the big names such as Borland, Netscape, Creative Tech, and Microsoft — is an entry for The Howdy Company.

  3. Expand the entry for The Howdy Company. You then see your program name and, below that, an entry for the Recent File List and another called Settings.

+ Second, a flag signals the old functions that used to read and write an INI file that they now will use the system registry. Your program's key becomes HKEY_CURRENT_USER\ Software\The Howdy Company\Howdy.

Add the following call to appear after the SetRegistryKey() call:

```
WriteProfileString (_T("SETTINGS"), _T("Howdy
    Stuff"), _T("Boy, Howdy"));
```

Run your program, and refresh the registry screen. (In regedit, press F5.) Click the "Settings" key to select it, and on the right panel, you see a value key called "Howdy Stuff"; its value is "Boy, Howdy". Notice the Default value is not set; you can put an entry in it by passing an empty string (not a NULL) as the second parameter to WriteProfileString().

Your program (or any other) can retrieve this value at any time, even after it exits and has been restarted. The keys and values are kept in the system database and are called *Persistent* data. To retrieve the value, use the call

```
CString str = GetProfileString(_T("SETTINGS"),
    _T("Howdy Stuff"));
```

To retrieve the default value, use an empty string (_T("")) as the second parameter.

Other useful registry functions appear in the accompanying table.

Function	Use
LoadStdProfileSettings	Extracts standard INI values including the Most Recently Used file list.
RegCreateKey	Creates a new key in the registry. If the key already exists, it is opened.
RegCreateKeyEx	Similar to RegCreateKey, except it temporarily locks the portion of the registry it is using. This is the preferred function.
RegOpenKey	Opens a registry key using default security values. Fails if the key does not exist.
RegOpenKeyEx	Opens a registry key using security mask provided by the calling function.
RegCloseKey	Closes the specified key. If the key is locked, this call unlocks it.
RegDeleteKey	Deletes a key and all the values associated with it. Fails if the key is open. In Windows 95, the key and all its subkeys are deleted. In Windows NT, the call fails if the key has subkeys.
RegFlushKey	Force writes the key and subkey values to the registry. Similar to fflush() for a file.

Part XI

The Microsoft Foundation Class

The Microsoft Foundation Class library is taking on a *de facto* role as the standard for development of Windows applications. Although MFC isn't the best class library on the market (Borland OWL is far superior), MFC isn't a *bad* library. MFC can frustrate you in many places, but, in the end, you'll be a better programmer because of the knowledge you gain in dealing with MFC.

I can't give you every object in every class in this chapter (or even in this book, if that was my only goal), so I present some of the most useful objects in MFC and a few tips for dancing around some of its vagaries.

In this part . . .

- ✔ **Application classes**
- ✔ **CObject — genesis of the classes**
- ✔ **Dialog classes**
- ✔ **Enabling dialog commands**
- ✔ **Tips for programming with MFC**

Application Classes

All the code in the Microsoft Foundation Class library is code you don't have to write. A basic application created using the MFC AppWizard includes six classes. If you select compound document support, the wizard adds an OLE container class.

The table summarizes the basic application classes derived from MFC. The sample names assume you created an application called Myapp, so substitute your application name where you see Myapp.

See also "MFC AppWizard" in Part II.

Class	Base Class	Purpose
CMyappApp	CApplication	Main application class. Contains InitInstance() where you would set initialization, read input arguments, and add document templates.
CAboutDlg	CDialog	Creates a basic About dialog box for your application. The class definition and functions are all contained in the main application file.
CMainFrame	CMDIFrame or CFrameWnd	Creates the main window for your application. If you created a multiple-document interface, it is derived from CMDIFrame. For a single-document interface, the base class is CFrameWnd.
CChildFrame	CMDIChildWnd	Creates the multiple-document interface client. This class is not included if you select single-document interface in the MFC AppWizard.
CMyappDoc	CDocument or CRichEditDoc	Supports the basic functions to create, load, and save a document. This is where you would add your special code to manipulate documents. The base class for a rich edit view is CRichEditDoc. Otherwise, the base class is CDocument.
CMyappView	*varies*	Creates the window to display your document. This is where you would add code for user interaction, such as editing text, listing records, and so on. The base class is the class you select in Step 6 of the MFC AppWizard.
CMyappCntrItem	COLEClientItem or CRichEditCntrItem	Creates the container class or OLE objects. These objects usually are read and saved using the document class. If you select None for compound document support in Step 3 of the MFC AppWizard, this class is not included.

The basic MFC AppWizard-generated application is a "program in a box." If you selected an edit view as your view class, you can compile the program without adding any code at all; run it; and begin opening, editing, and saving files. You have the basis of a utility program such as Notepad. You'll want to add code to make it perform your specific task, of course. The world doesn't need a plethora of Notepads; one per universe is quite enough.

CObject — Genesis of the Classes

Among the sparse printed documentation you get with the Developers Workshop is a chart of the Microsoft Foundation Class library. At the top of the chart you see a class called CObject, with its bar extending across the top. CObject is the ancestor of most of the classes in the MFC library.

Not all classes are derived from CObject, but chances are if the class accepts input from some device or displays something on the screen or printer, you can trace the class back to CObject.

CObject's constructor is protected, so you can't declare an instance of it; you can only derive classes from it.

See also "Constructors" in Part VIII.

Down the chart is CCmdTarget. Classes that accept messages generally are derived from this class, including CWnd, the basis for most of the classes that actually display objects on the screen. Dialog boxes, views, and the common controls all derive from CWnd and, consequently, from CCmdTarget.

If you are going to derive a new view or control, you should follow this sequence. Each derived class inherits the functionality of its parent classes, and much of the work in handling input and display is built into CWnd.

Dialog Classes

CDialog is the base class you will use to display dialog boxes. You won't declare an instance of this class directly. Instead, each of your dialog boxes will have a class derived from CDialog, in which you will write the specific code to handle your dialog functions. The dialog box you create in the Resource Workshop is simply the template that CDialog uses to create the box on the screen.

CDialog itself is derived from CWnd, and dialog boxes derived from CDialog are windows in themselves. The following chart shows the MFC classes derived from CDialog. All of the classes in the chart inherit CDialog's functions and variables.

Class	Use
CCommonDialog	The base class for the Windows common controls. The common controls are CFileDialog, CColorDialog, CFontDialog, CFindReplace, CPrintDialog, CPageSetupDialog, and COleDialog.
CPropertyPage	The base class for property sheet (tab) and wizard pages. Use CPropertyPage together with CPropertySheet, which serves as a container for the property pages (CPropertySheet is derived from CWnd).
COlePropertyPage	Base class to display the properties of a custom control. Classes derived from COlePropertyPage are used to build the Properties dialog box for a custom control.

See also "Dialog Boxes" in Part IV.

Get to know CDialog. I consider dialog boxes a very important part of an application and tend to spend a lot of time on them. A well-designed, efficient dialog box makes the user feel at ease in using an application.

Member functions you will find useful are listed in the table below. These functions all have public or protected access, so you can override them to add your custom code.

Member Function	Purpose
DoModal	Creates a modal dialog box from your template. Override this function to pass the dialog box class any parameters it needs when the dialog box is created.
NextDlgCtrl	Moves the focus to the next control in the dialog box. You may want to call this function when the user has typed the maximum number of characters permitted in a control or has performed a required action.
PrevDlgCtrl	Moves the focus to the next control in the dialog box.
GotoDlgCtrl	Moves the focus to a specified control. If you want the cursor to land in a control other than the first control in the dialog box, include a message handler for WM_SHOWWINDOW and call this function from the message handler. Calling this function from OnInitDialog doesn't work.
GetDefID	Returns the resource ID of the default button in a dialog box.
SetDefID	Sets the default button for a dialog box. The default button is the button specified when the user presses the Enter key while in a dialog box.
EndDialog	Terminates the dialog box. You may include a return value in the call to this function. The return value is passed back to your code that called the dialog box.
OnInitDialog	Initializes variables and controls.

Member Function	Purpose
OnOK	Override this function to perform any value checking before closing the dialog box. Called when the user presses the OK button. If you simply return from this function, the dialog box will not be closed. To close the dialog box, call the base class OnOK() function.
OnCancel	Override this function to provide a confirmation that the user wants to cancel. Called when the user presses the Cancel button or hits the Esc key.

Dialog Command Enablers

Often in creating and coding a dialog box, you need to limit a user's input. If you press a button to perform a function but the function doesn't work because the program is in a certain state, you may want to disable the button. Doing so gives some feedback to the user and heads off the "Why doesn't this work?" complaint.

You could write a function to do this and call it from every message handler in your class, but what if the program state changes between messages? How do you update the buttons before the next user input? Have you ever noticed that buttons in Microsoft programs seem to enable and disable themselves? The functionality is in Visual C++, and I consider it a serious deficiency of MFC that Microsoft chose not to include it in the CDialog class.

 You can add command enablers to your dialog boxes by using a couple of undocumented Windows messages, WM_KICKIDLE and WM_IDLEUPDATECMDUI. Don't bother looking these up in the InfoViewer — they aren't there.

First, add message handlers for these messages to your message map. You'll have to add these manually; the ClassWizard does not have them in the CDialog class message list.

```
ON_MESSAGE(WM_KICKIDLE, OnKickIdle)
ON_MESSAGE(WM_IDLEUPDATECMDUI, OnIdleUpdateCmdUI)
```

Next, add functions to handle these messages. Again, the ClassWizard will be of no help to you. For WM_KICKIDLE, add this code:

```
void CMyDialog::OnKickIdle()
{
    AfxGetApp()->OnIdle(-1);
    OnIdleUpdateCmdUI();
}
```

(continued)

(continued)

```
void CMyDialog::OnIdleUpdateCmdUI()
{
    UpdateDialogControls((CCmdTarget*)this, TRUE);
}
```

Magically, your dialog box now handles command-enabling messages.

Suppose you want to enable a Hangup button if the modem is on line or disable it while a file is being transferred. Add the command line to your message map:

```
ON_UPDATE_COMMAND_UI(ID_TELCO_HANGUP,
    OnUpdateHangup)
```

and the message handler function to your dialog class:

```
void CMyDialog::OnUpdateHangup(CCmdUI * pCmdUI)
{
    pCmdUI->Enable (sender.GetModemState());
}
```

The `sender.GetModemState()` would be a function in your modem handling code, of course, and `ID_TELCO_HANGUP` would be the resource ID of the Hangup button. The button is enabled or disabled depending upon the returned value.

Again, you'll have to add the `ON_UPDATE_COMMAND_UI` message handlers manually.

MFC Programming Tips

I hate programming. It's not as interesting as my previous occupation as a newspaper reporter, often repetitive, and, all too often, very frustrating. So why do it? Because programming has been my bread and butter for a long time, and over the years I have developed some techniques to reduce the tedium and frustration. Besides, I enjoy the satisfaction of seeing others use programs that I have developed and the freedom to improve those programs. With an off-the-shelf application, you're stuck with the programmer's ideas and hung out to dry with the application's bug.

A library such as the Microsoft Foundation Class helps a lot. The basic coding is one for you, and you quickly can get into the meat of your application.

Still, even with MFC, you're going to find yourself standing on your head to make things work. Build on your own work as well as that of other programmers. You can find a lot of literature on the Microsoft Foundation Class (there has to be), and don't hesitate to crack a good tutorial on MFC.

Approach programming and MFC methodically. One invention of the wheel is enough (they're all *round*). The following tips may help you in program development:

✦ Try small development projects to work out coding problems. Rather than compiling and linking large projects while trying to make troublesome functions work, create a smaller project just to work on that problem. When you get the code to work, transfer it to your larger project.

✦ Keep a notebook. Whether a disk file or a printed notebook, this record will be invaluable in later program development. When you work out a programming problem, transfer the code snippet to your notebook along with any observations or quirks you noticed.

✦ Build a library of functions you use often. The IDE allows you to create a library project, or you may want to include functions or custom controls in a dynamic link library and load it with your applications. DLL projects also are possible with the IDE.

✦ Keep an eye on the developers' section of the Microsoft Web site, `www.microsoft.com/win32dev`. This site has lots of articles, some dating to before the introduction of Windows 95, but new ones appear from time to time. Even so, the existing articles contain a number of programming tips.

✦ Develop your own sample programs. Many of the sample programs that Microsoft provides suffer from the ivory tower syndrome. The projects are written for the specific example rather than how you might use the code in real-world programming. You may find adapting Microsoft's sample code into your own applications difficult.

For example, I keep a project called CONTROLS that uses all the common controls as I would use them in an application, not just a dialog-based program written specifically for a single control. I keep copies of it for the Borland and the Microsoft IDEs, which are the two major environments I use. When a new version of an IDE is released, I test it against this project (and a couple of others), make whatever adjustments are necessary, and include notes for that release. When I need the code, I lift it out by using the clipboard and drop it into my current project.

Techie Talk

Abstract Class: A class that is intended to be used as the base for other classes. An abstract class is created by setting the address of a virtual member function to NULL. Thus, an abstract class may not be created directly.

Accelerator: A keyboard sequence that mimics a menu selection.

Accelerator Table: A resource containing the accelerators. A program may have several accelerator tables, which may be loaded on demand or associated with particular menus.

ActiveX: The new specification for OLE (Object Linking and Embedding). ActiveX is used to create compact, reusable controls.

Animation Control: A control to display successive frames of an .AVI file to represent motion. Files used with this control may contain only a single video track and an audio track. If the audio track is present, it is ignored.

AppWizard: A sequence of dialog boxes in the Visual Studio that takes you through the steps of creating the basic files for an application. There are several application wizards in Visual C++, each intended to generate a particular type of application.

Array: A contiguous sequence of data elements all of the same type.

Automatic Variable: A data element that is created when it is needed and destroyed when no longer used. Automatic variables may have a very limited scope, such as within a loop.

Automation: The process of exposing an object or function to external processes. This is a key feature of ActiveX controls.

Base Class: A class used as the building blocks of another (the derived) class. A derived class inherits the functions and variables of the base class.

Bitmap: An array of bits that describe the colors of an area of the display or printed page. May be stored in a file (.BMP file).

Bookmark: A marker in a Developers Studio edit file that lets you move to it quickly. Bookmarks may be accessed from the Edit menu by typing Alt+F2 or by selecting them from the edit toolbar.

Breakpoint: A debugging point in a program that causes the debugger to halt the execution of a program at the point just before it is to be executed. Breakpoints are used to halt execution so the program state can be evaluated.

Button: A control that simulates the action of a button. Pushing it with the mouse causes a message to be sent to the window or dialog on which it is located. A button may be part of a toolbar. Most dialogs have at least one button.

Check Box: A true or false control used in dialogs. When selected, the check box contains a check mark.

Class: The primary means of encapsulating data and functions in C++. The same as a structure in C programming.

Class View: The pane of the Workspace Window that lists the classes in a project. The pane is accessed by pressing the ClassView tab on the window.

ClassWizard: A Developers Studio tool for creating and modifying classes in a project. This wizard may be used to add message handlers and some member functions.

Combo Box: A common control that combines an edit control with a list control. Often features a drop-down selection box.

Common Controls: A set of standard controls available to Windows programmers through a library provided by Windows. Common controls benefit users by presenting a consistent look and feel to programs and dialogs.

Common Dialog: A set of predefined dialogs available through a Windows library. These include dialogs to select fonts and color and to open and save files and printer dialogs.

Compile: The process of converting the written program code into object code. The linker uses the object code to generate the executable code that can be understood by the computer.

Component Object Module: A specification defining the basics, construction, and use of an object. COM is at the basis of ActiveX and OLE, and programmers may create their own object modules.

Constructor: A member function of a class that is called whenever the class object is created. A constructor has the same name as the class and may not have a type specified. Used to initialize class members upon construction.

Context Sensitive Help: A message handler that puts an application into Help mode on demand. The function retrieves the Help ID of the object under the help cursor and spawns WinHelp to display the help item for that object.

Control: A programmable component intended to produce a specific result. Button controls, for example, generate a Windows message when they are pressed.

Custom Control: A programmer-defined Windows control. Custom controls give a program a distinctive look and feel as opposed to that offered by common controls. A number of commercial custom control libraries are available, or a programmer may roll his own.

Debug Version: A copy of a Developers Studio program containing information needed by the debugger. Visual C++ normally maintains a Debug and a Release version of a program.

Debugging: The process of finding and eliminating errors in a project. Often accompanied by wailing and gnashing of teeth.

Desktop: The view of tools and icons presented by a program. The screen first created when Windows is started is commonly referred to as the Desktop, but a program may create its own. The Visual C++ screen is an example of a program desktop.

Destructor: A member function of a class that is called automatically when the class is destroyed or goes out of scope. The destructor is a convenient place to free heap memory allocated by class functions. It has the same name as the class but is preceded with a tilde (~).

Dialog Box: A window that encapsulates controls through which a user interacts with a program. A dialog box may be used for complex data entry, or it might be as simple as a message box.

Dialog-based Application: An application that uses a dialog box as its main window. Such applications usually do not use views (but they may, as in the case of the record view) and generally are limited to specific functions.

DLL (Dynamic Link Library): A collection of functions that is loaded by an application at runtime. DLLs reduce program size and free up memory because they may be loaded and unloaded on demand. The common controls and common dialogs are examples of functions encased in DLLs.

Dock: A position on the main frame of a window where a moveable toolbar may be placed.

Dynamic Linking: The process of using DLLs to call library functions rather than including them in program code. With dynamic linking, a library may be loaded and unloaded as it is needed.

Edit Control: One of the common controls used to accept text input from a user or to display information. An edit control may be static, in which case it cannot accept user input.

Exception: A C++ construct that allows programs to gain control when an unexpected event occurs that normally would cause the program to terminate.

File View: A pane on the Workspace window that displays the files in a project. It is accessed by pressing the FileView tab of the window.

Group Box: A rectangular control used to visually group other controls. It is a static control used for visual effect only.

Harbor: A position on the window frame where a toolbar may be docked. A harbor may be the top, bottom, or one side of the main window frame. Multiple toolbars may be docked in a single harbor.

Header Control: A small window placed above columns in a control or view. It normally contains a label for the window and may be resized by the user. A header control is used in the "Report" mode of a list control.

Header File: A file that contains definitions and prototypes for a C or C++ program. This file usually is given the extension .H or .HPP.

Hot Key: A key combination a user may press to perform an action quickly. A hot key generates a WM_HOTKEY message, which is interpreted by the application to perform a specific action.

Icon: A graphic representation of an object, usually used to refer to the image that represents a program on the desktop or in the Start Menu.

IDE: Integrated Development Environment. An application that includes the tools and controls necessary to develop other applications. These usually include at least an editor for writing program files, a compiler, and a debugger. The Developers Studio is an example of an IDE.

Image List: A collection of same-sized images, usually bitmaps or icons, used by a program or control. Because all the images are the same size, they may be accessed by specifying an offset into the file, such as with an index variable.

Info View: The pane on the Workspace window showing documentation and help files available from the Developers Studio. It is accessed by pressing the InfoView tab in the Workspace.

Label: A named execution point in a program, denoted in C and C++ by adding a colon to the name. While it has some benefits in debugging, labels have virtually disappeared from C and C++ programming techniques.

Linking: The process of collecting all the object modules generated by the compiler and creating an executable program or library.

List Box: A Windows control that allows a programmer to list items in a defined area. Depending upon programming code, a user may select one or more items in a list box to be acted on by the program.

List Control: A new control introduced in Windows 95 that features different display modes: icon, small icon, list, and report. List controls are used throughout Windows 95 to display folder contents.

Loop: A section of repeating code that, ideally, should have some means of terminating itself. Loop constructs provided by C and C++ include the `for loop`, the `do loop`, and the `do-while loop`.

MAPI: Messaging Applications Programming Interface. The collection of functions that enable a program to access Windows messaging functions, including creating and modifying mailbox entries.

Member Function: A procedure that is included as a member of a class. Member functions may be called directly by other class members or externally by specifying the class object. Member functions may have access rights imposed on them, such as private, public, or protected.

Member Variable: A data object that is included as part of a class definition. Member variables generally are declared protected or private so that only member functions may access and modify them.

Menu: A list of items that are used to generate commands for an application. Menus are placed on a menu bar, from which submenus may be made to pop up when an item is selected.

Message Box: A standard box used to alert a user of a program condition or to provide feedback to the user from the programmer. In Microsoft Foundation Class applications, it is invoked by using the `AfxMessageBox` function.

Message Handler: A function that implements a program's response to a Windows message. When placed in the message map for a dialog or application, it is invoked automatically when the message is received.

Message Map: A collection of statements that define what messages an application or dialog will respond to. The message map includes the message ID, type, and the address of the message handler, although some of these may be defined in a macro.

Microsoft Foundation Class: Microsoft's implementation of a class library for C++ programming. It is provided with Visual C++.

MRU: The Most Recently Used file list. An application maintains this list to simplify retrieving recently used documents. The MFC AppWizard generates the basic code to maintain an MRU in the Windows registry.

Multiple-Document Interface: A specification originally defined by IBM for creating client classes to manage more than one document. MFC contains full support for MDI, and the task of setting up the client and views is handled by the MFC AppWizard.

Multithreading: The process of setting up multiple execution points in a program. A multithreaded program may be performing several tasks at once, and the technique is used by programmers to perform time-consuming tasks that do not require user input.

Object Code: The numeric code that is used as commands by the central processing unit. Compilers generate object modules containing object code, which are then joined by the linker to resolve addresses.

Operator: A C or C++ symbol that causes a specific block of code to be generated by the compiler. The plus operator (+), for example, causes the compiler to create the code to add to its two operands.

Output Window: A window in the Developers Studio that provides feedback to the programmer. In the distribution configuration, it is at the bottom of the IDE and is used to provide messages from the IDE tools as well as from programs that are being tested.

Pointer: A variable that contains a reference to another variable. A pointer contains the address in which a data element is stored. C and C++ functions cannot directly modify variables in a calling function, but if the programmer passes a pointer to the variable, it may be modified indirectly.

Popup: A menu or window that normally remains hidden until it is invoked by some action of the user. In the case of a menu, it usually is a submenu that remains hidden until the user presses a particular item on a main menu. In the case of a window, it is a special type of overlapped window normally used for message boxes, dialog boxes, and other temporary windows.

Print Preview: A special window that emulates the context of a printer. In applications generated by the MFC AppWizard, code is automatically generated if the "Printing and Print Preview" box on Step 6 of the wizard is checked.

Process: A program that has been loaded into memory and is either executing or ready to execute. Until an executable file has been read into memory, it is an ordinary program.

Program: A file containing the code to execute a particular application. When it has been loaded into memory and is ready to run, it becomes a *process.*

Progress Bar: A common control used to indicate the status of a time-consuming procedure. This is represented by an elongated rectangle with a color bar that moves across it. The color bar is under the control of the application.

Project: In the Developers Workshop, the collection of files — source, header, resource, and so on — that comprise the code to build an application. A project is contained in a workspace, which may include several projects.

Property Sheet: A dialog-based tab control that was introduced with Windows 95 and is used throughout the operating system. The property sheet holds one or more property pages, which are accessed by the user by selecting the proper tab.

QuickWatch: A dialog that contains an edit control where you may enter an expression to evaluate and a spreadsheet area that displays the contents of the item you entered. Use this to examine or modify a variable during debugging.

Radio Button: A common control that works much like a multiple choice answer. Radio buttons are grouped together, and within the group only one of them may be selected at a time. Selecting a button automatically deselects the previous.

Registry: A database introduced with Windows NT that is used to store configuration information for the operating system. It also may be used by applications to store configuration information. The Windows API contains a number of procedures for registry operations.

Release Version: A non-debug version of an application. This version is maintained by Visual C++ and may be invoked by selecting "Set Active Configuration" from the Build menu.

Resource: In a Windows application, this is binary data added to the executable file to describe icons, cursors, menus, dialog boxes, bitmaps, fonts, keyboard-accelerator tables, message-table entries, string-table entries, version data, and user-defined data.

Resource View: The pane of the Workspace window that lists the resources that are included in a project. It is accessed by selecting ResourceView from the Workspace window tab.

Rich Edit Control: A common control that encapsulates the features of the edit control but includes functions that allow user or program selection of fonts, colors, type size, and so on. It is most commonly used as the base of a view class.

Scroll Bar: A Windows interface that converts mouse or keyboard input into values used by an application to shift the contents of a window horizontally or vertically. It is commonly implemented using the scroll bar control.

Single-Document Interface: A document interface that lacks the code to display more than one document or record at a time. The contents of the document may be visible in multiple views, however.

Slider Control: A common control that operates much like the sliding volume controls on audio equipment. The control may be moved by user input and its relative location read by an application and used to perform a particular application. Examples of slider controls used horizontally and vertically may be seen in the Windows volume control application.

Sockets: A network programming interface originally specified for the Berkeley Scientific Distribution (BSD) implementation of UNIX. Sockets are intended to relieve the programmer of the details of network communication.

Source Code: The (sometimes) human-readable form of program code. The compiler used the source code to generate the equivalent object code for use by the linker and computer.

Spinner Control: A common control used to accept user input for a value that can be incremented or decremented. It gets its name from the way the value in an associated edit control spins up or down when a button is held down.

Static Linking: The process of including library code in the executable file of an application. Statically linked code becomes part of the program and does not require the presence of a DLL to execute. Static linking may dramatically increase the size of a program.

Static Variable: A data element that is created when a process is launched and remains throughout the life of the program. It retains its value unless it is changed by the program.

Status Bar: The informational strip at the bottom of a main window that contains indicators for time, messages, and keyboard state such as the current setting of the Num Lock, Caps Lock, and Scroll Lock keys. The MFC AppWizard generates the code to display a status bar if you check the "Initial status bar" box on Step 4 of the wizard.

String: An array of type `char`. C and C++ do not have data types for text, so strings are implemented by declaring an array of `char` large enough to hold the text. In the Microsoft Foundation Class, you may use class CString for strings of variable length.

String Table: A list of values, IDs, and captions for the strings in your application. The string table is a convenient place to store program text, and if you are planning versions of your application in other languages, you may change the language by substituting string tables.

Switch: A C and C++ statement that performs the operation of a multiple if-then-else statement with some restrictions. A switch statement contains a set of "cases," which must be constant values. Also, the test expression in a switch statement must evaluate to an integer.

Tab Control: A common control that operates much like the tabs in a notebook. It was introduced with Windows 95 and is the base control for property sheets.

This: The egocentric identifier for a class. Often, class members have to refer to the class instance, but they have no way of knowing the variable names the programmer used when they were created. So C++ provides a "this" operator that permits a class to refer to itself. It's always all lowercase.

Thread: The execution point of a process. Every process has at least one thread and may contain several.

TLA: Three-Letter Acronym. Well, they are so common in the computer world, isn't it proper for TLAs to have their own TLA?

Tool Tip: A common control that provides the small popup window giving tips on how to use a control. Typically it is invoked when the mouse cursor is held over a control containing a tool tip.

Toolbar: The collection of controls encapsulated within a single object to make it easier for the programmer to manipulate them. A toolbar usually contains an array of buttons, but it may hold any Windows control.

Tree Control: A common control introduced with Windows 95 that displays data elements in a structured fashion, much like the branches on a tree. The views in the Workspace window are examples of tree controls.

View: A description of the way a document or record is displayed on the screen. Views may be constructed using appropriate controls, such as the edit, rich edit, list, or tree controls. In MFC, base classes are available for views that do not correspond to common controls, such as CRecordView for database objects.

Watch: A tool to display the value of variables while a program is being debugged. Watches are placed in one of four Watch Windows in the Developers Studio. Local variables may be modified in the watch window, but global variables may not.

Wizard: A special case of the property sheet that allows users to access pages in a preset sequence rather than randomly.

Wizard Bar: A Developers Studio toolbar that provides quick access to class members, functions, and declarations. In the distribution configuration, it is placed immediately below the main toolbar.

Workspace: The area of the Developers Studio that contains projects and their configuration. A workspace may contain only one or a number of projects, which may be of different types. For example, a single workspace may contain a Visual C++ project and a Visual J++ project.

Index

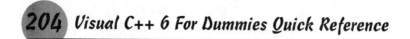

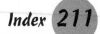

IDG BOOKS WORLDWIDE BOOK REGISTRATION

Register This Book and Win!

We want to hear from you!

Visit **http://my2cents.dummies.com** to register this book and tell us how you liked it!

- Get entered in our monthly prize giveaway.

- Give us feedback about this book — tell us what you like best, what you like least, or maybe what you'd like to ask the author and us to change!

- Let us know any other *...For Dummies®* topics that interest you.

Your feedback helps us determine what books to publish, tells us what coverage to add as we revise our books, and lets us know whether we're meeting your needs as a *...For Dummies* reader. You're our most valuable resource, and what you have to say is important to us!

Not on the Web yet? It's easy to get started with *Dummies 101®: The Internet For Windows® 95* or *The Internet For Dummies®*, 5th Edition, at local retailers everywhere.

Or let us know what you think by sending us a letter at the following address:

...For Dummies Book Registration
Dummies Press
7260 Shadeland Station, Suite 100
Indianapolis, IN 46256-3945
Fax 317-596-5498

BUSINESS AND
GENERAL
REFERENCE
BOOK SERIES
FROM IDG

COMPUTER
BOOK SERIES
FROM IDG